THE ART OF MINDKEEPING

The Secret to Activating Wisdom, Healing, and Spiritual Fulfillment through Lumen Consciousness.

Stacey McCann

Published by Mindkeeping LLC
5 Manatee Court
St. Augustine, Florida 32080

ISBN: 979-8-9898286-0-9

The content of this book is to provide information, examples, and
testimonials for educational purposes only and does not constitute
consultation or professional advice. Each situation varies, and this
book offers a general guideline for individuals interested in the subject
matter.

The Secret to Activating Wisdom, Healing, and Spiritual Fulfillment
through Lumen Consciousness

CONTENTS

INTRODUCTION

Imagine if what we thought about ourselves was untrue and what we have learned is inaccurate. Where does that leave us? How do we return to a new track we were unaware of?

Mindkeeping isn't just about my story. It is our story. It is the story that we are waking up to. It is the journey you long for but have yet to start. It is the new beginning of you in your most happy and brilliant form. It is beyond the illusion of what you think you are and into the truth of what you are: a mystical, magical, creative being in a human body. As you follow along, you will find your storyline. As for me, this is how it all began.

From as early as I can remember, I had a heightened consciousness or awareness that was way beyond my years. There was my adult voice talking inside my head. It wasn't there all the time, but when it was there, it was profound enough for me to pay attention.

As I got older, I began to realize a different kind of awareness. It was an awareness that was beyond me yet was still part of my experience. It started one day while walking home from school with my friends. I lived about a mile from the school, and about halfway through the journey was Robin Hood Park. Robin Hood Park was our hangout. That's where we went to play. They had camp counselors in the summer, and we made things like lanyards and did arts and crafts. The park had a lot of sycamore trees, which we called itchy ball trees because they had these balls on them. We used to jump up to grab the balls and throw them at each other. One day, we were jumping for our itchy balls, and something strange happened when I reached for mine. I felt a pinch. Then, another friend grabbed theirs, and I felt another pinch. *"What was that?"* I wondered. Was I imagining that, or was the tree talking to me? The message was clear: *It hurts when you pull things off me.*

My friend Cheri lived right across the street from the park, so when she went home, I did the rest of the walk to my house in solitude. Still perplexed by what had happened, I jumped at tree after tree, pulling leaf after leaf with the same results. It hurt. I wasn't imagining it; I was experiencing it. Whenever I pulled a leaf off, I experienced an unpleasant sensation like a pinch.

I understood what the tree felt I felt, but the difference was the tree didn't get mad. It just felt the pinch and moved on. I was fascinated that the trees had no emotions. They could feel the pain, but they didn't react. Truth be known, if you pinched me, I would yell, scream, or have some visceral reaction. I was fascinated by the tree's response because it taught me there was no separation between us. Even though I was human and the tree was a tree, we somehow shared an experience. The tree was just matter-of-fact about it. It was what it was, and it moved on. The trees became my first great teachers, and I revere and respect them greatly.

Another time, I was outside playing in my backyard and suddenly became fascinated with my hands. I saw my hands, as I did daily, but it was in a new light this time. I looked in wonderment as I recognized the claw- like objects as tools that were not part of me but rather borrowed for the time being. I knew in that instant that I did not belong in this body and that it was a loaner. It was like a special suit, and I was in amazement.

I was like a kid in a candy store who wanted to share this remarkable finding with everybody. My friend was there, and I told her, "Check this out; isn't this the coolest thing you've ever seen?"

"What," she asked.

"Our hands, look how they work, they're like claws. Check out how they move. Isn't that so cool?"

She replied, "What are you talking about? So, big deal, they're hands."

I could not understand how she could not comprehend what I was saying. Didn't she see what I saw? She was in the body too; why couldn't she see the funny costume?

As a young girl, I always felt something was hovering over my head. It was a presence, but I didn't know what it was. It felt like something was watching over me, like a parental presence or an authority. In one way, it was good, but in another, it made me self-conscious and afraid of making a mistake. Part of me knew that this was the connection to my inner self, my more extensive awareness that told me about the trees and the hands. But then I realized that only some people are in touch with this connection.

The more I noticed that I was different, the more confused I became about this presence. I knew it would not hurt me, but it made me feel stupid and inadequate. I wished that it did not bother me, but it did. It was hurtful, and I was growing more uncomfortable with each experience. I hated that I was like this because it made me feel vulnerable. I did not know how to deal with it. I would ask myself why I felt so overcome with feelings.

What is wrong with me that I have all these emotions to keep choking down? Why can't I be normal like everybody else? I put on a tough exterior to compensate for how fragile I felt. It did not take long for me to think that nobody could relate to or understand me, and most importantly, I could not understand myself.

It took me years to figure out that I was empathic. I was feeling my feelings and emotions and the emotions and energy of all the people around me. I did not know what it was or how to decipher it then, so I thought nobody liked me. I believed it was my fault when I felt inner turmoil or anger. I thought I had done something wrong and everybody was mad at me. I had no clue what was going on. I only knew that if so many people felt this way about me, something must be wrong with me. I learned very early on that if I wanted to feel safe, I had better please the people around me and make sure they felt happy.

I never really felt that I could be myself. I always thought that I had to hide. In April 1987, I moved from New Jersey to Arizona with my husband and baby daughter. I loved it. It was the Old West. I didn't know a soul and didn't have to live up to anything I believed someone else thought I should be. My husband was an over-the-road trucker and wasn't home much, so most of the household responsibilities were on me.

After our second child was born, I was exhausted. I was tired of working part time , tending to the kids, cleaning the house, cutting the grass, and everything else needed. So, when I put the kids down for a nap, I took one too. Sometimes I would nap, and other times I would meditate. I started meditating a few years earlier, but I needed to improve at it. I was just too hyper. I could not relax or control myself. There were times, however, when I was just so tired, it was easy to let go, and on this one day, something extraordinary happened.

I was lying on my bed, taking deep breaths, trying to relax. I went through my ritual. Relax my feet, my ankles, my shins and thighs. Relax my hips and abdomen and so forth. Usually, by the time I got to this point, I was so antsy, I could not go any further. Today was different. Today, something happened that was so profound, such a defining moment, that it would change my life forever.

As I was lying there, I could hear a deep, vibrating sound resonating around me. *Vur, vur, vur* in and out. I do not know how to describe it other than like a giant spaceship you might see in a sci-fi movie. It is unlike any sound I have ever heard in my usual state. I couldn't move my body either. I didn't feel scared, and I didn't feel this was a bad thing. Although, I was unsure if I was even in my body anymore. It was weird but peaceful.

The next thing I knew, a light appeared, and Jesus stood beside me. In my mind, I was thinking, *This is weird. Why is Jesus standing here?* I hadn't called or asked him to appear in my meditation; he was just there.

We didn't speak to each other, nor did we have to. There was just an understanding between us. It was nice. I was curious to know how long it lasted. It seemed like only a few minutes, but it could have been more. Upon parting, Jesus touched my foot, sending a jolt of electricity through my body and the top of my head. The current of electricity was so intense that it shook my body and rattled my teeth so hard that I thought it might have cracked them.

The only thought that came to mind was *Whoa, that was cool; what was that all about?* I didn't understand it then, but I knew it was an initiation. (Side note: When I went to the dentist, the hygienist said, "You have some cracked teeth." I thought, *Holy shit!*)

In 1991, my youngest child was born. He had breathing issues and was borderline asthmatic. The doctor said if his symptoms did not improve, he would have to take medication and be on breathing treatments. With two other children, a job, and no medical insurance, this was not an excellent option for me. I had to figure out a better way, so, on a wing and a prayer, I thought to place my hands on him to draw out the infection, and it worked! Every time he started to get sick, I put my hands on him, and he was better by the next day. What blew my mind was he was only six months old and too young to be swayed or influenced.

I was fascinated and determined to understand what I had done and how I had helped him. I sought out healers, spiritual leaders, and people who provided alternative modalities. As luck would have it, Arizona was a hub of spiritual activity and a playground for my insatiable curiosity. It did not take much looking to find somebody or something that screamed spiritual, holistic, New Age, or any other free-spirited modality that was out of the ordinary. I was thrilled. Here I was, finally, around what I thought were like-minded people who understood me. I was in my element, and it felt good.

I joined a group that met once a week to talk about all things spiritual. They introduced me to new ideas beyond what I had already read or experienced. I enjoyed the group and took to the lessons immediately, but as time passed, I realized I was outgrowing them. It was now time for me to move on because I wanted more. I wanted more information and insight to know what I had done for my son.

I tried everything under the sun, allowing myself to be poked, prodded, read, bled, oiled, steamed, manipulated, needled, and so much more in search of answers, only to conclude that nobody knew any more than me.

I set myself in the right direction but could not yet see clearly. I still did not understand much about myself, spirituality, and God. I felt that I was running in circles, and after all this time, I still did not know how I helped my son.

I refer to the following seven or eight years as the "Are you my mother?" years. If you remember the children's book by that title, it is about a baby bird that sets out to find his mother. He looks everywhere and asks everybody, "Are you my mother?" That is what I had become: the little bird looking for my mother or, more accurately, myself.

I was working at a pool company selling pools when I met Judy. Judy was originally from New York, and we hit it off like pizza and pepperoni. We talked about spiritual ideas that interested us and books we had read. She liked working with the pendulum and was studying to be a hypnotherapist. I told her everything I had done and that I had been meditating for years, but I was so hyper it was hard for me to focus. She suggested that she try her hypnotherapy on me. She needed the practice anyway, so why not use me as her guinea pig? Of course, it took no convincing on my part.

After a session or two, I felt a floating sensation. I said, I felt like I was floating. Judy said that's what you are supposed to feel.

That's what your spirit feels like when it is expanding, and suddenly, I had some focus and understanding because I had a reference point of what I was supposed to feel like.

I still needed my direction, so I decided to do my homework. I was not entirely in the dark. I had experience with different healing modalities, but I was ready to take it to the next level. I explored in search of any particular modality I felt drawn to. I also wanted to know what other practitioners were doing. I wanted to know what was working for them and why. I wanted to know how they learned to do what they do and what drew them to it. I wanted to know if all "healers" had the same or similar philosophies and/or personalities. I wanted to know who, what, where, when, and how to figure out what I was doing and what I had done to help my son.

I started with past-life regression, thinking it could give me insight into what I might have done in the past, but it was not helpful. Next, I went to my friends who were astrologers, tarot readers, numerologists, herbalists, and aromatherapists. I expanded from there to venues that they recommended and so on. Whenever I tried something, I tried it repeatedly with different people unless it turned me off or I felt it was not good for me.

Over the years, I tried and experienced so many modalities, and this was just the tip of the iceberg: alpha biotics, acupuncture, acupressure, aromatherapy, ayurvedic medicine, miscellaneous herbal detoxes and sweat lodges, naturopathic medicine, homeopathy, chiropractic both palmer and network, homeopathic dentistry, energy work in a multitude of disciplines including Reiki, healing touch, spiritual healing, intuitive healing, fractal healing, therapeutic touch, chakra balancing, chakra clearing, chakra alignments, shamanic healing, Native American healing, crystal healing, rock healing, electromagnetic healing, quantum healing, creative visualization, feng shui, flower essence therapy, ear coning, chelation therapy, kinesiology, hyperbaric chamber therapy, art therapy, sound therapy, red light therapy, reflexology, craniosacral therapy, Rolfing, rife therapy, massage, biofeedback, sound therapy, and toning.

I have had psychic readings, tarot readings, angel readings, soul readings, palmistry readings, past-life readings, numerology readings, astrology readings, aura readings, I Ching, and teeth readings.

I realized everybody had an opinion or a philosophy, be it Wicca, the Kabbalah, Buddhism, Tibetan Buddhism, Egyptian god/goddess, Mayans, Aztecs, Atlantis, Lemuria, Aliens, Native Americans, or different branches of Christianity.

My experience was that some modalities and ideas worked, and some did not. There were some that I liked and incorporated into my daily meditation and routine and still use today, and others that I thought were just crazy bullshit.

Once you know something, you can't go back and *un*-know it. If

I did, that would not be very responsible on my part. Once you know something, you choose to own, accept, or deny it. It is one thing not to know. It's another to have the knowledge and intentionally not use it. I knew. Now, it was time for me to shape it into something tangible. To do that, I had to determine how I had gotten to this point in my life, so I asked myself what prompted me to look for answers to my questions and how I came up with the solutions.

If I could explain this to myself, I could explain it to others. All I had to do was remember where I came from. This idea seemed logical to me. The curiosity to understand my experiences is what prompted me in the beginning.

I had so many questions. Why did these things happen to me? Were they random? Does everybody feel this way? I did not think so based on my past experiences. Other than seeing an occasional psychic or tarot reader, I did not have anyone I could trust to discuss this information, so I read books to find answers.

In my early years of spirituality, I read a lot. I read anything related to the occult, healing, philosophy, religion, energy, and inspirational or thought-provoking books. I read Edgar Cayce, Carlos Castaneda, Napoleon Hill, Neale Donald Walsh, James Redfield, Louise Hay, Raymond Moody, Dannion Brinkley, Silvia Browne, Bette Eadie, Caroline Myss, Deepak Chopra, Andrew Weil, Joseph Campbell, Helen Blavatsky, Plato, Aristotle, the Bible, the metaphysical Bible, Osho, *A Course in Miracles*, and the list goes on.

I agreed with some of what I read, but not all. My thoughts were drawn based on my feelings about what I was reading. I kept an open mind if it felt right and logical. If it did not, then I let it go. One book that I particularly liked was *The Tibetan Book of Living and Dying*. In a nutshell, the book states that the answer to living is in dying. That made so much sense to me that it was a turning point, not only in the way that I now incorporated that teaching into my lifestyle, but it also made me look deeper into another concept. What if there were no books?

I thought, what would happen if we were on our own spiritually? What if there were no Jesus, Buddha, Muhammad, or other great teachers who came before us? What if there were no books like the Bible, the Bhagavad Gita, or the Koran to follow? What if there were no churches to go to and no sermons to hear? How would we differentiate between what is physical and what is mystical? How would we know the difference between what we learn and what is instinct? How would we know which feelings are appropriate and which are not? Could we determine Divine guidance from worldly influence? Would we evolve spiritually without knowing it? How would we find our moral compass if somebody was not telling us what it should be? If we had no spiritual direction, would we figure it out ourselves, and if so, how would we do that?

The concept intrigued me so much that I decided to put the books down and find the answers to my questions solely by trial and error. I wanted to know what was right for me, and I wanted to know how to access myself. I would apply different methods to see if they had any effect on me. Sometimes, I would combine methods, and sometimes, I would make them up myself as I went along. It was an experiment, and I was Dr. Frankenstein.

The more I learned about myself, the more I wanted to know. The more I learned about myself, the more I knew about the people around me. It was like solving a puzzle or playing a video game. Once I reached a level of understanding, a new level would open up for me. It was the ultimate golf game in the sense that just when I would get to the point that I was so frustrated and wanted to quit, I would hit a shot or receive an insight that was so good I had to keep trying.

If I lived by my own spiritual compass and moral code, I would have to create a solid foundation to build upon, meaning I had to define a philosophy to live my life by.

There were so many schools of thought, but none were an exact fit for me. If I was going rogue, it better be based on something I believed in and could stick to. I realized that everything I did and would continue to do was to understand myself better, so it would only make sense that my philosophy would be about my relationship with myself. With that understanding and commitment, my philosophy was born.

"There is only one relationship, which is the relationship with myself. All other relationships stem from that foundation." I have lived by this philosophy since its birth approximately thirty years ago. It has never let me down and is as solid today as it was at its inception.

Now that I knew what I was all about, I needed a practice or method to incorporate into my philosophy. What were my building blocks, and how could I prove they were accurate? The one constant in my life was self-reflection. I have been reflecting and meditating my entire life; however, I was only sometimes aware that I was doing it. It took many years before I discovered that pensiveness, daydreaming, and imagination are all forms of meditation and self-reflection. Another essential building block was self-discipline. I had to dedicate time to myself daily to make measurable progress. Sometimes, it was challenging, but it was worth it because it made me feel good. My final building block was practice. As the saying goes, how do you get to Carnegie Hall? Practice, practice, practice.

The more I practiced, the stronger I became in so many ways. First was focus and clarity, then intuition and insight, then understanding, health, and so on. This practice is a process that went on for years, and as it progressed, I progressed. As my method evolved, I evolved. What used to take me years to accomplish I was now completing in months, weeks, days, or hours. Something had changed. The energy was different and more accessible, and I was fortunate enough to be tapping into it.

The more I tapped in, the more questions I had, so I applied the same concept. I asked myself, what if there was no God as we know it? Who would we pray to? How would we pray? If we were not asking God for help and divine intercession, would we be capable of creating it ourselves? Would we have power beyond our human capabilities and be good people if no one was looking?

I experimented again, only this time taking the external concept of God out of the equation. The one fact I could not deny based on my experience is that I could feel a force and a physical change in my mind, body, and spirit depending on how I directed the energy of my meditations. I also realized how I could change my negative experiences into positives by adjusting my energy frequencies; however, I could only do it internally, not externally. What I mean by this is that I had to be accountable for what I felt or how I reacted to everything in my life. If I tried to externalize it, the process would not work. I had to learn to process information from my heart, or feelings, instead of my head, or thoughts. I understood that this change in processing information made a significant difference in my level of intelligence by increasing my consciousness to a greater level of understanding. The higher I went, the easier it was to understand myself, and the more I understood myself, the more I understood that we are all connected to and a significant part of this force we call God.

Like the wizard in *The Wizard of Oz* , we pull the strings behind the curtain. We create our reality but need to elevate our minds to comprehend it. As we evolve, we understand that we are the force that we call God, not in the sense that we are the all-knowing God but in the knowing that we create everything in our lives and reflect it into the world. Whether it pleases or hurts us, this is our birthright and path of evolution. It is our initiation into wholeness or holiness. It is now up to us to run with it.

CHAPTER 1

Mindkeeping

M y spiritual journey didn't start later in life. I was born this way. I was born with a heightened consciousness and an unusual sense of self. At times, it was good, but most times, I didn't understand it, and it scared me.

Most children have spiritual experiences and connections to other-worldly things. It is natural to have "imaginary friends" and know something about others they didn't tell you. Most people outgrow this as life starts filling in for spirit. For others, it never goes away. You mask it behind something else to fit in. That's what I did. I just pretended it wasn't there. I learned to distrust myself and put my trust in others so I wouldn't have to deal with what I felt or knew. I ignored the signs because they were painful. I ignored the signs because I wanted to feel loved and fit in. I ignored the signs because I felt isolated and misunderstood when I acknowledged them.

I disliked this part of me, and I was intrigued at the same time. I was not fond of how it made me feel, but I loved knowing things. I hated feeling overly sensitive, yet I loved feeling connected to a force far beyond me. It was not a religious connection. It was a spiritual pull. It was a force so strong within me that I could not have stopped it if I had tried, and believe me, I have tried many times. I equate it to trying to stop a wave from the ocean.

My hands and body are no match for that kind of power. It is ridiculous even to consider it, so instead of fighting, I decided to try to go with it, like a person on a life raft on the ocean. It has been an up-and-down ride with a lot of thrills and sorrows.

Some days were excellent, and some days sucked. Sometimes, I wanted to quit, and that force would pull me back in. *Why?* I would wonder. *What the hell is this all about? Why can't I be normal like other people? Why do I care so much? Why can't I go about life without constantly obsessing about it, not in the sense that I care about the outer me but obsessing about my inner mind?* The constant internal conflict to feel and heal, feel and heal. Why? What was I doing it for? Who was I doing it for? How could I turn it off? Where was the off switch?

The answer is I am doing it for me. My life is about me, and your life is about you, and the only person who can change your life is you. You already know that, though, so what will I tell you that you don't already know? I'm telling you that you are not what you think you are. You are an evolving species. You are a human evolving into the next generation of consciousness called Lumen, as in light. You are entering Lumen be-ingness, and the pull or what you may experience as feeling stuck, wanting more, gaining purpose in life, feeling depressed, hurt, or pain is your way of evolving without consciously knowing it.

It is your pull to a higher power. It is your pull to higher intelligence. Like my obsession to feel and heal is my way of gaining more intelligence. The more I have, the more I want. The more I have, the more I know nothing, and the more I have, the more I know you because we are all connected to the same fabric, even though you experience yourself as separate from me. As artificial intelligence is to Alexa, evolution is to us. Evolution is our nature, and conscious evolution is our birthright.

Putting the process of Mindkeeping into words was one of my biggest challenges. After all the years of practicing, it had become automatic, and when others wanted to know more, I had to think about it. How did I do that? How do I explain that? What do I name this practice that is more experiential than explainable?

This process took years. At first, my explanation was so technical, I even bored myself explaining it. I was trying to make it more than it is.

I thought you would feel it was more credible if it was complicated and scientific, but it's not. It is practical and easy. I like it that way; I don't like complex. I want the meat-and-potatoes, cut-to-the-chase, bottom-line approach, so here it is.

I created Mindkeeping because I wanted answers. I wanted to know how to change the way I felt. People on social media or podcasts tell you that you feel the way you do because of your childhood, upbringing, or environment. They may even offer you a seminar that helps explain that your mother didn't give you enough love or what have you. Yes, it is accurate, and it is helpful. I am not disputing that, but it doesn't make you mindful. It tells you the reason without finding a solution. If you know you feel unloved because your mother didn't give you enough attention, now what? Where do you go from here? Do you go home and yell at your mother for not giving you enough attention? Of course not, as that doesn't help you solve the problem; it only enables you to recognize it. To solve or resolve, you have to evolve.

Mindkeeping evolves you past the hurts and pains of the physical world and moves you back into your spirit. When you live your nature as a spirit in human form instead of a human with a spiritual connection, your life significantly improves because you work with your soul instead of against it. You begin to understand yourself as a system instead of just a body. When the system connects, it gives you access to information, wisdom, and knowledge you can't reach now as an individual part.

Mindkeeping is the practice of self-discovery and change. It takes what is already there and improves it by simply addressing your mind as a system instead of just thoughts. Your mind is not what you think it is. Your mind is a system similar to a cell phone. Have you ever had an old cell phone? Why did you finally upgrade it? Because you wanted to have the latest, greatest, fastest, most efficient model to make your life easier

Very few, if any, of you still use a flip phone. You want the best technology. You don't want to settle for a second-rate product. You want better, faster, and more efficient. The same should apply to you. Why settle for a mediocre human mind when you can upgrade to your better, faster, and more efficient lumen mind? Both belong to you; however, one is old and outdated, and the other is better and more efficient. Technology has moved us into the twenty-first century; isn't it time you catch up?

WHAT IS MINDKEEPING?

Mindkeeping is a meditative technology, or in other words, it is meditation and technology rolled into one. It is a practice like meditation with built-in technology to help you heal yourself by transcending the limitations of the human mind.

Mindkeeping can bring you closer to God, whatever that is for you. Be it comfort, peace, healing, wisdom, understanding, confidence, or love. It gives you the courage to change and the freedom to create what you want, when you want, and how you want by training your mind to reach higher levels of consciousness.

Mindkeeping is easy. It is like tending to your house by housekeeping or your money by bookkeeping. You are watching and managing what comes in and out of your mind, which monitors what comes in and out of your life. It is the practical application of mindfulness because it not only calms your mind but also changes it from being stuck and limited by your physical five senses and expands you into your sixth and higher senses. Higher senses mean higher intelligence and the ability to see and create beyond the physical realm. It's like a computer. You may not know exactly how it works, but you know that you input the information you want and trust that the answers come back to you. When that information is no longer needed, you delete it and start again. You upgrade to a more efficient model when the computer or information becomes outdated. Mindkeeping is as easy as that. You don't have to know precisely how it works. Just follow the process and you will achieve the results you want. Everything you do starts within your mind, so knowing and understanding how your mind works as a system is essential.

MINDKEEPING IS A HUMAN TECHNOLOGY

Technology has changed the world, but it has not changed you. Why, with all the technological advances in the world and beyond, how could you forget to include yourself? It's ridiculous to think that humans don't need technology too. We keep dumbing ourselves down as our machines smarten up. We have almost taken ourselves out of the mix of everything. How often do you actively participate in your own life? After all, if you don't catch up with artificial intelligence, will it eventually be more intelligent than you?

Do you do online dating? Do you swipe left and right to find your perfect mate or partner for the night? Why do you put more faith in a program or app than yourself? Does Alexa tell you it is five o'clock on Friday and the weekend started or notify you when it's time for you to reorder a product? Do you buy everything on Amazon because you want it tomorrow, no matter what it is? Why? Because it is convenient and easy. The easier life becomes, the lazier you become because there is an app for it. What about you? Where is the app for you? Where is the technology for you? What do you need to move you out of the dark ages of your mind and into the new, improved, faster, better, more advanced version of you?

Mindkeeping elevates your mind and makes you organically more intelligent. AI dumbs you down by giving you someone or something else's answers, but OI (organic intelligence) makes you smarter by giving you your answers. This human technology makes you the driver of your life instead of the passenger in someone else's life. Mindkeeping moves you beyond the human mind's hurts, pains, beliefs, ideas, actions, and re-actions and into the wisdom, knowledge, understanding, and confidence lying dormant and waiting in your lumen mind. It also advances you from third-dimensional linear thinking to the more progressive fifth-dimensional empathic thinking. OI is as easy as updating an app on your phone. The only difference is that you are the technology that is now updated.

MINDKEEPING IS EVOLUTION

Life is a constant cycle of evolution. Can you think of one thing that stays the same? You change whether you want to or not. It's human nature. Even when you are not paying attention to it, it still happens. Think about when you were born. You were not consciously aware of it or a week, month, or year later. You didn't stay the same; you changed. You grew, and as you grew, you evolved to childhood, puberty, and adulthood. Your body grew, as did your knowledge and ability to learn new things.

Most of that evolution happened without you putting much thought or focus into it. You were on autopilot, allowing it to take you in any direction. What if you could steer that ship in a specific direction? How would you grow? Would you increase your intelligence and knowledge? Would you give yourself superpowers? What would you do if you realized you were limitless? If you had the same intelligence as Alexa, what would you input? What would you want to know more about? If you knew that you could evolve as quickly as you update your cell phone, would you be willing to try it?

The world around us is evolving faster than we are. Think about how technology has grown in the past fifty to a hundred years. When my father was a child, his family was among the first to own a TV. When I was a kid, color TV had just started, and there were only a few channels to choose from. Now, there are hundreds of options, from live TV to streaming. In 1978, I was a telephone installer for New Jersey Bell Telephone Company (which no longer exists). It was a big deal for two reasons. The first was I was female in a male-dominated trade. The second is that job no longer exists because technology has made it obsolete. In my lifetime, my first real career was extinct because technology made it so.

Do you know anybody with a hardwired telephone in their house? How about that second line for the teenager? No such thing. The portable phone took over the hard-wired telephone, and the cell phone took over the mobile phone, and who knows what is next? Technology moved it all forward and made life easier and, in most cases, better for all of us.

That is just one example. You can think of multiple ways technology has changed our lives. The point is that technology has helped humans evolve, and everything has developed except humans. Not in the conscious sense, anyway. You have developed physically but not consciously. If you did, you would understand that what you think and believe about yourself causes pain. As you consciously evolve your mind, you experience life from a higher perspective. From this perspective, you can input the information that propels you to the most advanced version of you. Isn't it time to catch up to our innate technology.

PRACTICAL APPLICATION OF MINDFULNESS

Mindkeeping is the practical application of mindfulness because it changes your mind as you practice. Meditation, yoga, and stress relief will calm your mind but not change it. Although you will temporarily feel calmer, it doesn't change the underlying issues that caused the stress in the first place. Changing your mind changes the frequencies of your consciousness, which helps you stay happier for extended periods. An example is when you decide to take a mental health day. You may get a massage, take a hot bath, or binge-watch movies on the couch. Whatever it is, you are happy to be in your space and to give yourself some much-needed downtime. You feel relaxed, rejuvenated, and comfortable until the kids come home from school and all hell breaks loose. One child needs a ride to dancing school and the other to football practice.

They begin to fight over who gets dropped off first. You have to be in two places at once quickly and go across town through traffic. You then have to drive home, make dinner, and turn around to pick up the kids. When you pick them up, one of them tells you they volunteered to bring in cupcakes for the party at school tomorrow. Your stress level is through the roof, and you want to escape but can't. You feel stuck.

Now, what do you do? You have two options. Calm your mind or change your mind. Calming helps you temporarily, but you still repeatedly deal with the same problems. Changing lets you resolve the issues by giving you greater insight and ideas to deal with problems permanently. Let's face it: life can be stressful, so why not use the tools to make it easier? Changing your mind is the conscious way to change your life positively. Is there anything more practical than that?

BEING MINDFUL

What does it mean to be mindful? Most people I talk to believe it is being aware of their thoughts and paying attention to their actions. Although that is true to a certain degree, it doesn't encompass the meaning of being mindful. If you are mindful, you pay attention to and cultivate the relationship between your mind, body, and spirit. It isn't about paying attention to how you breathe, how you sit, or what you ate for dinner last night. To truly live mindfully is to live as a spirit within the physical body.

Spirit is your nature; physical is your experience. Mindful is consciously understanding that your mind is more than your thoughts. It is your spirit personified in the physical. Being mindful helps you to understand yourself from that perspective and live from that higher octave of yourself. When you live from your spirit, you are mindful, not mindless. Mindless does not mean that you don't have a mind. Mindless means you must pay more attention to what comes in and out of your mind. When you are mindful, you make life happen consciously. When you are mindless, life occurs randomly.

TO BE MINDFUL INSTEAD OF MINDLESS

Mindfulness is not about reinventing the wheel. It is about taking the wheel and making it better and more efficient. When you direct your mind in the way you want, it merges with universal consciousness (lumen consciousness), giving you information and knowledge you didn't previously have access to. Mindkeeping enhances your life in all directions simultaneously. As you improve your mind, you improve your life.

For instance, let's say you want to feel more confident. Expanding your mind makes you feel more confident emotionally and in all aspects of your life, such as your finances, career, and relationships. Mindful moves you forward; mindless keeps you stuck.

SOME OF THE BENEFITS OF MINDKEEPING

You Know

What a great feeling it is to know. I like knowing. Knowing helps me get through life in the easiest way possible. Of course, not everything I know is sunshine and roses. At least having an idea that something is going down helps me to prepare for it so it isn't so difficult when it happens. One thing I know is how I feel, and knowing how I feel gives me the power to understand how you feel. Knowing how you feel is my business. If I don't know, I can't help you, and I like helping you. It makes me feel good, and I enjoy watching you grow, too.

Knowing how you feel allows you to change the things you don't like. That makes intuition an essential and valuable tool. Think about it. You put more thought into what you like or don't like to eat than what or how you want to live. You may think nothing of passing on the broccoli at the buffet table but can't grasp the idea of walking away from a relationship that leaves a bitter taste in your mouth.

I like knowing when someone is lying to me. That's not to say that I am 100 percent accurate all the time, but when I feel uneasy, I walk away. That makes me feel good about myself. That's not to say that person is bad. It's just not someone I choose to be around or deal with.

I like knowing the right thing to say to someone when they need a pick-me-up or giving them tough love when they need a little push. I love knowing that I am being true to myself, which means I am being true to you too.

I like knowing what it feels like to trust myself even when uncertain. I like knowing that I always have a choice and deciding what that choice will be for me at any time.

I like knowing if something is off in my mind or body to address it before it becomes a significant issue. I like knowing I will always be okay, no matter the diagnosis or circumstances. I like knowing peace and living a peaceful life. I like knowing that if I don't have a solution for my problems, I can create one. Knowing adds a layer of confidence to everything you do, and who doesn't want or need a little more confidence?

Become a Better Person

Who wouldn't want to be a better person? I know I do, and I know I have. When I was younger, I didn't have the integrity or wisdom I have now. Some of that came with age, but most came from Mindkeeping.

I have become a better person in every way. Things that I did in my past I no longer need to do. I no longer look to others to feed my needs because I now fulfill them myself. For instance, when I was young, I felt very starved for attention, so much so that I would feed that need at all costs. It didn't matter if it was not good for me. What mattered was someone gave me attention. That attention made me feel loved and cared about until I realized the attention was at my expense. I was doomed as long as I looked to someone else to make me feel special, which trapped me in an illusion that became more important to me than my self-respect, self-esteem, self-value, and self-worth. I didn't care about me. I cared about whoever would give me that attention or that feeling that I was important, valued, or special.

My life hinged on ensuring those people had everything they needed to make me feel good. What a waste of time and energy. I allowed that need to take everything away because I didn't want to or know how to take responsibility for myself.

Once I took responsibility for myself, everything changed for the better. I became more intelligent, mentally and emotionally. I could see things before they happened or recognize the red flags to detour from things or people that weren't good for me.

I learned to be kind and to respect myself. With self-respect, no one can walk on you or make you do what you don't want to do. My self-esteem improved, as did my confidence and belief in myself. My integrity improved, and I no longer needed manipulation to get what I wanted.

I've gained trust in myself and know when to "hold 'em" and when to "fold 'em" because I know everything will work out in my best interest, and it does. Whether it is how I want it to go doesn't matter because the bigger picture will reveal itself to me.

My finances increased because my self-worth and value increased. I found my voice and became able to communicate my actual wants and needs, knowing that I was being heard and acknowledged.

My vision kicked in, and I could see the whole picture instead of a slice of the truth. My insight gave me the wisdom to move forward with understanding and compassion.

My talent and skills for healing skyrocketed as my empathy increased. My ability to know what others need to move forward and help them heal from the past gave me the power to be a better mother, sister, friend, healer, mentor, and colleague. I am so proud of what I have become. I am proud of the person I am and the person I am continuously evolving into. I love myself and the better version of me that I am. Do you want to be a better person, too?

Self-Discovery

When I started, I had no interest in self-discovery. I wanted to be spiritual. I wanted answers. I wanted to know how I knew things. Self-discovery never entered my mind. What is self-discovery anyway? I know who I am. At least, I thought I did. How about you? Do you know who you are? When you look within, do you know what you are looking for or supposed to be looking for? I certainly didn't. I was a prime example of someone who knew nothing about myself. I believed that to be a good person, I had to be what everyone else wanted me to be.

So, I became what my husband wanted, what my kids needed, what my boss expected, and what my family had determined was right for me. I had no mind of my own, no opinion that I thought mattered, and no voice. I didn't stand up for myself and did whatever was necessary not to rock the boat. I tried to make others happy, but it was all at my expense. That is not to say anyone intentionally tried to hurt or harm me. Of course not, but I would suffer in silence because I could not think, speak, or act independently.

I see this over and over again in my clients. They are miserable because they don't know who they are. They don't know what they want. They don't know where to begin to find themselves, and they are angry about it. They resent others for holding them back, yet they don't know what they want or need to move forward. I even have clients who are racked with grief over the death of a loved one, not only because they miss them but because they don't know who they are without them. They have not had to stand on their own two feet, and it scares the heck out of them.

That's not to say they aren't resourceful. They are some of the most intelligent, most accomplished people I've ever met; they just lost their identity.

Reclaim Your Identity

I don't know a soul on this earth that doesn't struggle with their identity. After all, isn't that counterintuitive to what you've learned? Don't act like a big shot; be a team player, and do what is in the best interest of all. You should sacrifice yourself for the greater good, so where is your individuality in that? It's challenging and confusing. You want to be a team player, but if you are unique, you subject yourself to ridicule, judgment, and feeling apart from the whole instead of part of it.

How do you reclaim your identity, be your own person, and still fit in? Have you taken the time to ask yourself? Who better to answer any questions about you than you?

What am I about? What is my character? What do I believe? How am I supposed to act? What do I expect from myself, and what do I perceive is expected of me? What do I want, and when I get it, will it be enough for me? Am I comparing myself to others? Do I measure up? If not, why don't I, and what can I do about it?

You have the answers. It would help to ask yourself the questions and be patient to receive the answers. The one question I always ask those seeking my help is how do you see yourself, and how do you want to be seen? You'd be surprised by how many people see themselves in a negative light. When asked what they think their strengths are, it almost always points to doing something for someone else. Such as "I'm a good mother or a good friend." It is rarely said, "I am sure of myself, confident, able to express myself in a way that I am heard, acknowledged, and respected." Why? Because you don't know who you are.

Men have one set of rules, and women have another neither is fair or honest to who you are or what you want. I have clients who have said they never knew who they were. Others have always told them what to do and how to act. They didn't act independently; they didn't know how to. They didn't want to upset their family, friends, or coworkers. They thought it was better to suck it up than to speak up for what they wanted, which they couldn't do anyway because nobody told them what that was.

It is a vicious cycle of doing for others at the sacrifice of yourself. That is not to say that you don't want to help others. Of course you do. However, you can't give what you don't have. Too often, you overextend yourself to ensure the other person is happy. Their happiness is your goal, and as long as they are happy, you are happy. Right? Wrong. Their happiness is not your responsibility. You are existing and doing what you think you are supposed to do. Why? Because you don't have an identity or you had one and lost it.

I understand this dilemma. I have lived it myself. My family, society, and environment dictated most of who I thought I was. I lived and did for everyone else because that is what I knew. In my mind, I didn't exist outside of them. If they wanted something I didn't want, I would give in to what they wanted. My likes were their likes; my hobbies were their hobbies. It was as if I was the passenger in everyone else's life but my own.

I went along mindlessly. I wouldn't say I agreed with or liked it, but I didn't know how to escape it. I was angry. Angry at others for making me this way. Angry at them for bullying me and coercing me. I never thought at the time that I was afraid to have a mind of my own.

Losing one's identity happens all the time. I have client after client tell me they last knew themselves in high school or younger. They don't feel carefree anymore. They are afraid to take chances or try new things, not because of failure but because they don't know how to get out of their way. Once taught, they start to find themselves again, and life opens up in new and exciting ways. They feel better about themselves. They understand the stories that led them to where they are now and have the tools they need to move forward in a happy, healthy, confident way that uplifts them in every direction.

Find Your Purpose

Clients always come to me because they want to know their purpose. What am I here for? What am I meant to do? Truthfully, I don't know what you are here to do; you do. I can help you along the path and guide you in the right direction. I can even make suggestions based on your energy or what I am picking up from you, but ultimately, the choice is yours.

I struggled with finding my purpose for years. I kept thinking it was something that I had to do or accomplish, only to realize that it's not something you do but something you are. Your purpose is to be GREAT. To be more significant than you are now. Ever-growing, expansive, and evolutionary. Moving beyond what you think you are into the truth of what you innately know you are. To do this, you have to know yourself.

Mindkeeping will help you find your greatness by allowing you to find yourself. So, what makes you great? What does your soul want to share with the world?

Your purpose is to be greater than you are now and find that which makes your heart sing when you are doing it. It's whatever moves your spirit, whether in an art form or just being randomly kind. It is constantly being respectful and kind to yourself and open to new ideas and possibilities. It is learning to feel first and think second instead of vice versa. It is to transform from physical linear thinking to abstract mystical feeling continuously. It is to find your unique expression of life and way of expressing it without fear or care of judgment. It is putting yourself first so you have the resources to help others.

To sum it up, your purpose is to be greater than you are now and live in that magical space that uplifts you and those around you. It doesn't matter what form it takes. I always say I am the same person whether teaching a crowd, shopping in the supermarket or just hanging out watching TV. My greatness remains the same; only sometimes, I am more focused on it than at other times.

Discover Happiness

Somebody asked me what is the one thing that everyone wants. I said, I have been asking myself that question for years, but most tell me they want happiness. When asked what that means to you, the usual response is, "Happiness is having a good family and friends."

That's a valid answer; however, most people I ask already have those things and still want to be happier. What if you took that statement out of the mix? What if you couldn't respond with good family and friends and had to focus on something else? Can you answer that question? Most people can't because they don't know what it is or can't define it. How can you have happiness if you don't know what that is for you? You can't.

Not knowing creates a dichotomy. Either you have what you want and are not happy, or you don't have what you want and are not satisfied. What is it that you want or need to make you happy? Is happiness what you are searching for, or is it something else? How much time do you put into finding what you want? Most people don't put much time into finding the answers, especially if it requires real effort.

When teaching, I like to go around the room and ask each person their favorite color and number. Their responses are instantaneous. Blue fourteen because my son was born on the fourteenth. Another will yell out green and seven. The next is yellow and three. Without pause, they have their answers ready to share with the rest of us. They are ready and eager to share until I ask the next question. What does happiness mean to you? You would be amazed how that question stops everyone in their tracks. Why? Because they are so used to making their happiness about others that they don't know what that means for them as individuals.

Of course, having a happy family and great friends is rewarding, but this is not about them. It is about you. What makes you happy as an individual? Is it singing, dancing, creating, tinkering, gardening, learning, or something else? It can be a million things, and there are many variables; even with that, you still don't know how to answer the question. Neither could I. That's what prompted me to ask the question in the first place.

It all started because I wanted to paint my bedroom a new color. I thought, what color would make me happy? Well, that opened a Pandora's box. The next thing I knew, I pondered my favorite color, which led to my favorite number and what would make me happy. Within this cul-de-sac of my mind came the realization that I am more connected to my favorite color and number than I am to my happiness. Yikes! I realized I had better shift my priorities because if I can't answer that question, how can I achieve lasting happiness? My happiness is more important than any color or number. After all, who cares if my bedroom is blue, green, or purple? Who cares if my favorite number is six, nine, or ninety-six? Those things don't affect my life, but my happiness does. It affects not only my life but everyone and everything in my life, too.

What do you want and need to make you happy? Some will say to win the lottery. Is that really what you want? It could make your life easier in some ways, but is that the answer to your happiness? Some will say good health. Is that all you need? Does good health make you happy? If you regain your health, is that all you need? Some will respond by saying they want solutions to their problems only to take the advice and never act on it. Others wish to have answers but need to ask the right questions.

You ask about love and money. You ask what your future brings. You ask if that guy or girl you have your eye on is the right one for you. You don't think to ask about you. You ask about things and outcomes. You don't want solutions; you want a storyline with a happy ending. You want somebody to write your narrative. Not because you are lazy but because you don't know how to write it. You have not learned how to think independently for yourself without feeling guilty or wrong about it. If you continue that course, you will never find happiness or peace of mind.

Do you want peace of mind? What is it, and what does it feel like? If you knew how good it felt, you would strive for it. I know I do. I prefer it to stress, anxiety, and all the other drama happening worldwide. However, it takes time to have peace of mind. It doesn't happen overnight. You have to put some effort into it. The effort is well worth it, but let's go beyond that. What do we all want that encompasses everything? What is the one thing that can make us happy and gives us the time, energy, money, and ability to do what we want? Freedom!

I believe freedom is the answer. Freedom gives you the power to do what you want, when and how you want, without question or pause. Freedom from the limitations of guilt, worry, fear, pressure, responsibilities, burdens, and obligations. Freedom to experience yourself and what you can do without judgment of right or wrong, good or bad.

Freedom detaches you from the duality of the physical mind and into the unity of the nonphysical mind. You can be who you want, say what you want, and express what you feel in any way, shape, or form that pleases you and does no harm to others. It is the freedom of being without boundaries while consciously experiencing life. Freedom knows no boundaries and creates true happiness. Freedom is your highest, most divine expression of you in physical form.

Find Your Greatness

What's your greatness? Mine is self-discovery. It took me time to find that out. I thought that greatness meant I had to do something big or grand, but isn't doing something you love and are passionate about enough? I think so.

Find what you are good at and what makes your heart sing, and I guarantee you greatness is behind it. It doesn't have to be a grand gesture. It has to be passionate, and the way to uncover your passion is to look within yourself. Many of you have yet to have the opportunity to explore this part of you, while others start and stop and start and stop again and again. I will warn you that looking within is not always the most comfortable feeling, but once you get past the discomfort, the truth will quickly reveal itself to you.

Greatness can be a struggle. Not in the way you would imagine; most people say they embrace greatness when, in truth, they do everything they can to avoid it. Some can only see their shortcomings, so embracing greatness is something they can't emotionally handle until they work on themselves while others know they feel something great inside, but they can't seem to bring it to the surface. I just had this conversation with a friend of mine. She feels she is supposed to do something bigger in her life. She wants to help others and be of service, but she needs help to define it. She can feel it but can't visualize it. She can't see it because she hasn't looked beyond her physical self. The answers do not lie within the human mind. They are in the lumen mind. When you only see yourself from your human perspective, you become stuck in that perspective, which is limited by physical beliefs and patterns. In her case, she believed what she thought or wanted wasn't as important as what others wanted for her. She didn't see herself as an individual with her wants, needs, and desires. She saw herself as insignificant, without a voice, and unable to make decisions for herself.

For instance, she came up with an excellent idea for a business. Something she loved and would have been great at, but her mother disapproved. Disapproval happened to her time and time again. She thought that if her mother didn't think it was good enough, it must not be good enough. After all, as children, isn't that what we want: their approval? Listen to your mother and father. Respect your elders, and don't question what they say. They know what is best for you and what you need, but do they?

They do their best with the information they have, but most of your parents won't know what is best for you after you reach a certain age. They may project what they want or think is right for you, but how many of them are living the lives they want? They, too, do what they've learned or believe is the right thing to do. Of course, I am not talking about character or morality; those are separate issues. I am referring to personal expression and individuality.

When you lose your individuality, you lose the power to make choices. You do what others want instead of what you want for yourself because you don't trust yourself or it's easier than arguing.

Decisions are scary. You fear making mistakes. You allow others to make those decisions for you, blaming them if it doesn't work out. The crazy thing is that the more you make your own decisions, the fewer mistakes you make because you make decisions based on what is suitable for you rather than someone else. That's not to say that others don't have the best intentions. They do; however, no one can stand in for you. You are leading your life, which means creating your own identity.

Who am I? That question can be overwhelming when you don't know the answer.

Greatness isn't hard. It just has to be you being you in a way that makes you happy. Find what makes you happy. Look within and be willing to stand on your own two feet. It is when you step out of your comfort zone and into the awkward feeling of not knowing but trusting that you will end up in the right place at the right time.

Allow yourself the opportunity to find your voice and use it in a way that makes you feel empowered. Live knowing that being truthful to yourself is more important than if someone gets mad at you for it. Expect some resistance as you change, but don't allow that resistance to stop you.

Recognize the reference points along the way, and trust that you are on the correct path precisely as you should be. It is the new you in your most honorable and authentic form awakened from the most vulnerable and unsafe parts of you and into you that you have always wanted to be. Great.

Upgrade Your Mind

Upgrading is fun. Isn't it fun to buy a new car? How many more features does it have than your old car? How about a new TV, phone, or computer? Look at all the fantastic things you can do once you familiarize yourself with the new system. It's the same for you. Upgrading yourself is fun, and it is exciting to discover who you are and what you are capable of. My clients are happier than ever because they elevated their minds to higher levels of understanding, giving them the tools to live happier lives.

Not only does upgrading help you be a better person and have a happier life, but it also helps keep you safe. Just like the safety features on your car, upgrading makes you safer by alerting you to potential problems and dangers before they happen by sending signals to your higher senses. Your higher senses pick up information that your lower senses can't. As you upgrade, you become more protected in all avenues of your life. Be it physical, mental, emotional, financial, or spiritual.

How much more fun will life be when you find new skills and abilities you hadn't known existed? Imagine how empowering it is to have the clarity, focus, confidence, and ability to connect with yourself and others in a way you have not experienced before. All because you chose to upgrade your mind and download new information to improve your life and the world around you.

Heal

If you practice Mindkeeping, you will inevitably heal because you resolve your problems from their point of origin as you evolve.

Healing does not start in the body, so addressing the problems in the body from a physical perspective is not always productive. The diseases you feel within the body are not your real problems but indicators that you have something to fix within your mind system. The cause of the issues relates to how you see yourself and the world from your inner self, directly affecting how you feel in your body.

Healing starts inside the mind and runs through multiple layers, including your thoughts, emotions, and memories, before reaching the physical level. The body is denser than the other etheric layers, and it takes longer for you to feel the effects. However, even if you do not feel immediate changes, they are still happening. The healing (repair) process is easy, as you will learn later in this book.

Find Inner Peace

Finding inner peace may be the most essential benefit because inner peace encompasses all the other benefits. I have experienced that peace that passes all understanding, and I can tell you there is no more fantastic feeling of peace, love, and trust that compares. A calm mind is an intensely beautiful feeling that frees you from the inner chatter that creates fear, doubt, distrust, lack of confidence, and discord that you feel within you.

Mindkeeping helps you recognize and find that inner peace to turn the discord into confidence, trust, well-being, and happiness. When you have inner peace, you have outer peace. Whatever happens inside of you or whatever you are feeling inside of you is projected out into the world. If you have inner peace, you have outer peace. If you have inner turmoil, you have outer turmoil. Finding your inner peace is one of the best benefits of Mindkeeping.

CHAPTER 2

Spiritual or Psychic Development?

What is it you want? Do you like to learn about what and who you are spiritually, or do you want to develop your psychic ability? Some think they go hand in hand, but it depends on your motive. What is your reason for wanting to increase your psychic power? Do you want to predict the future or have Xray vision? If that's what you aim for, you will be sorely disappointed. If you develop your psychic power without the spiritual maturity to use it wisely, you may cause more harm than good.

If you develop spiritually, you will also develop psychically, but if you only grow psychically and not spiritually, you may be opening doors that are best left unopened. Awakening the mind without training can be like giving a child a gun without instruction or caution. The child might know what the weapon is and what it is supposed to do, but they need to gain the skill or maturity to use it properly. Energy is the same way.

Spiritual experiences can be fun and exciting because they take you beyond the limits of what you know. But if you are not careful, those experiences can backfire on you or cause collateral damage. If you develop yourself spiritually, you will have a much better chance of making mature decisions while increasing your psychic ability.

To be spiritual, you have to be spirit. Spirit is your nature. When you get to know your spiritual nature, it will expand in all areas of your life, including your psychic abilities. Practice knowing yourself, and you will start noticing changes in your life. You will begin to understand things you never understood before. You will start to feel compassion where you had none. You will begin to see beyond your physical eyes and hear with your inner voice. You will learn the language of light and speak telepathically to others on many different dimensions. You will find hidden talents and skills deep within yourself that you didn't know existed. All by simply learning to develop spiritually. In the long run, you will be much happier, more balanced, and able to know what doors to open and which to keep closed.

AWAKENING YOUR MIND

What does it mean to awaken the mind? Isn't your mind already awakened? How can you be awake and asleep at the same time? It doesn't seem possible, yet it is.

Awakening the mind is different from being awake. The awakened mind is like being the driver instead of the passenger of your life. The awakened mind is the driver; the sleeping mind is the passenger, meaning you do things without thinking. It's automatic and compulsive instead of conscious and intentional.

Awakening the mind is about change. Changing how you think from human to lumen changes the outcome of your life and experiences from random to desired. As your mind awakens, so do your senses, opening the door to higher levels of intelligence. This intelligence is a sixth sense, or universal consciousness in action.

The lumen mind is our true nature. You have learned that you are a human with a spirit, but you are genuinely a spirit with a human condition. Although fun and exhilarating, the human condition is also limiting and painful. The lumen mind is the master, the authority, and the creator. It is by far the greatest gift given to every human soul.

Imagine the things you can do when you tap into this gift. You can create a better future for yourself and the world around you. You can gain access to information that others don't know how to reach, thus giving you the tools to understand life at higher levels. You can hear what others are not saying, which aids in creating better relationships, be it personal or professional. You can heal the hurt and pain in your life by seeing and understanding why it is there and what it is there to teach you. You can find skills and talents you didn't even know existed, and you can find meaning and purpose. All in all, you become more intelligent, wiser, happier, and healthier. And that is just the tip of the iceberg!

When you understand what the lumen mind does for you, it becomes practical and necessary. Here's why. The human sleeping mind stays put out of fear. For example, a sleeping mind will remain in a bad relationship because it fears what will happen if it leaves. It dreads the unknown. Whereas the lumen mind is OK with moving on, knowing that the peace it will achieve is better than the conflict it is experiencing. It also understands that it created the drama as a means to move on and will consciously create a happier experience.

TRUE OR FALSE?

There are a million different ways to elevate your mind. As of late, you can find a holistic practitioner on every corner telling you how to do it or what they feel works best. How valid is all this information? After all, is someone who took a weekend course in energy qualified to be your spiritual mentor and guide? How do you know what is valid and what is not? Many people are out there selling their ideas, potions, and forms of energy. How do you navigate through it all?

When I started my journey, I was fortunate enough to have time. I worked in sales, and after the kids went to school, I scheduled appointments around the things I wanted to try. If I heard about a person with a holistic specialty, product, or procedure I wanted to try, I worked it into my schedule. I wanted to know what they did, how they did it, and what it would do for me. I tried so many things I can't even remember them all. Some were pretty mainstream, such as acupuncture, acupressure, reflexology, and network chiropractic, and others were more strange. I loved trying new things. I loved everything spiritual except church and religion because I didn't understand them. When I was young, I went to the Armenian Church. My father was Armenian, and my mother was not. We were half-breeds or *odars* , as they say in Armenian. We didn't speak the language, so I couldn't understand what they said. To me, the church was a feeling and nothing else.

Back in the 1980's, everything was about the New Age. New Age this and New Age that. I always thought that was ironic, as there is nothing new about the New Age. It is all recycled information put into a new form. In other words, it is a form of technology, and with any new technology, you have to determine what you like and what works best for you.

Elevating your mind is not a one-size-fits-all approach. It requires time and experimentation to determine what works best for you. What works for some does not work for others. Life would be dull if only one product could cater to everyone's needs. However, I would be OK with cornering that market.

Be kind to yourself as you explore your options. Remember that everyone is unique, not only in obvious ways but also in terms of energy. This uniqueness is where Mindkeeping comes into play. It doesn't matter what your energy level or level of comprehension is, as it works equally well for everyone and helps you stay on course.

WE ARE EVOLVING

If you want to heal, you have to evolve. If you want to change, you have to evolve. If you want to know the mysteries of the universe, you have to evolve. Everything you do and everything you will ever be begins by evolving. From the moment you are born until you die, you are evolving in some way or another. So, it only makes sense to pay attention to it.

Why do we evolve, and how do you evolve? The reason why is easy. We evolve to become better versions of ourselves and to reach the untapped potential and reality of what we are capable of. It's the same principle used in modern technology. Technology moves us forward and becomes a greater version of itself. For instance, it's like going from cellular 3G technology to 5G. 5G is faster, more reliable, and can access information that 3G can't. You are the same way. Think of it in terms of the dimensions of the mind.

Your physical mind uses third-dimension technology, yet it can have fifth and higher dimension technology. There is a big difference between the two, just as the significant difference between using a flip phone and the latest model cell phone.

In addition, evolving keeps you current with the technology around you. We have grown technologically as a race, but we need to grow emotionally enough to be sufficiently compatible with the technology created. Evolving progresses you emotionally and mentally to a new understanding and respect for who you are, what you are, and what you are creating, both as an individual and a species. Lastly, it makes you feel great because it syncs you with the vibrations and frequencies of universal consciousness. These frequencies create an inner peace that few know or have experienced for extended periods.

How to evolve is as easy as changing how you interact with yourself. You fail to change because you approach your life from only one perspective: that of thought, but by expanding that perspective into an emotional standpoint, you discover that you are so much more than just physical. You are metaphysical with the power to create new ideas, opportunities, and realities.

The great inventor Nikola Tesla said, "If you want to find the secrets of the universe, think in terms of energy, frequency, and vibration." That goes for you too. If you want to find the secrets of your universe, you need to understand that you are more than human; you are an energy system. To awaken and evolve as a human species, you must look beyond the human system and into the lumen system.

You have all referred to yourself in terms of energy in some way or another. You may have said you were high energy or felt tired with low energy. You may not like someone's energy and refer to them as having a bad vibe or negative. Sometimes, you just like someone for no apparent reason. What you are feeling is the vibrations and frequencies of their energy. You are already somewhat aware of it, but how do you measure and gauge this energy? You measure and gauge it through your feelings.

Feelings are your built-in radar system. The signals and frequencies tell you what is right and wrong in your life. You begin to evolve as you discern, interpret, and adjust the frequencies of these feelings. Evolving improves everything because it connects you to your higher senses and eliminates the need for outdated information that keeps you stuck in place.

Mindkeeping helps you evolve. It will teach you to recognize your feelings and adjust the outdated vibrations and frequencies or what you no longer want to feel into higher, more advanced energy. You heal as you change because to feel is to heal, and as you evolve, you resolve the problems that hold you back. When the energies reach a certain vibration and frequency, you move forward into higher states of consciousness. When you get to these higher states or dimensions, you change. You become more aware of yourself and everything around you. You start to think of yourself as part of a whole unit instead of just individually. You begin to feel what others feel and know what others know, which lifts you to want to be part of a solution. Evolution raises your compassion and desire to make yourself and the world a better place. This evolution is how you remember the love and goodness you are with understanding, power, and compassion beyond what the ordinary mind can imagine. It is where energy and feeling meet to take you to a new human paradigm of mindfulness and the evolution of your mind.

CHAPTER 3

Change

L ife has changed. Everything in the world has changed. Look at the past ten, twenty-five, or a hundred years. If everything around us has changed, how can we as a human species be stuck in the same mindset century after century? If technology can change, why can't we change too? But how do you change something if you don't know it needs changing? Even if you did know, where do you begin, and how do you do it?

My dad used to say, "Change is the name of the game." He was right. You have to change to move forward. If you don't change, you don't grow and you become stuck. Nobody wants to be stuck. That's why you want to change in the first place. The problem is that most people need to learn how to change. They change their things and convince themselves that's good enough. Well, that's not good enough because it still keeps you stuck. No moving forward, no changing, no evolution, just the same old you with newer and better things.

Change is in your nature. You certainly are not the same as when you were two years old. You've changed whether you were aware of it or not. Everything changes: nature, weather, people, places, ideas, and life. Life naturally changes, so it is time to figure out how to change along with it.

The way to change it is by getting to know yourself. You may be thinking, *I know myself.* But do you? I bet you know more about your spouse, kids, boss, friends, and foes than you do about you. I suspect you know more about what they are thinking and feeling than you do about what you are thinking and feeling. You learned to emphasize how they feel and neglect how you feel. How can you possibly know yourself without paying attention to yourself?

What you think and how you feel is the vital key to change. You are the only one who knows how you feel and the only one who can change that. Your feelings are your superpower. The way to access this superpower is to know yourself in a new way that takes you beyond your human senses and into your higher-lumen senses. In your lumen mind, you have access to information and knowledge you can't reach from the physical perspective.

You know things don't fulfill you, and you deserve fulfillment. Think how great life would be if it had meaning beyond responsibilities and obligations. Wouldn't going beyond the boundaries and coloring outside the lines be fun? What if you could be anything or have anything you ever wanted? What if you could find the real you inside yourself again by simply changing your mind?

What do I mean by that? Changing how you think, feel, and react opens the door to your lumen mind. Once these doors open, you can create the life you want. In other words, your life becomes more conscious and intentional and less uncontrollable and random.

By changing your mind, you consciously and intentionally create what you want based on what feels suitable for you. When you know what you want based on how you feel, it alters how you think and how you react. It's a chain reaction of positive energy with positive results, improving your life in every aspect.

WHAT DO YOU WANT TO CHANGE?

I always ask my students, why are you here? What brings you to class today? The answers vary, but the bottom line is they are there because they have something in their lives they want to change. After all, who doesn't? Everybody wants a change in some way or another, be it a situation, circumstance, belief system, relationship, finances, career, or self-image. Everybody wants change, but some don't know how to make it, so they stay stuck. If you are stuck in an unhappy place long enough, it creates more significant problems for you in the long run, such as stress, depression, and illness.

Unfortunately, many people do not know what they want to change. They think change is the answer, even if they don't know what that is. They may blame their circumstances on others, thinking that if others did things differently, it would solve their problems. You all know you can't change someone. You can only change yourself. So, what is it that you want to change? Do you want more attention or help from your spouse, children, or family? Do you want more time and money? Do you want to feel better about the way you look or feel? Do you want a lasting relationship or a new career?

What motivates you to change, and why do you want to change? Knowing your motive gives you purpose, and purpose gives change meaning. If you have a reason, you will probably be more apt to change, but there is still the chance of slipping back into old habits and patterns.

Some people make significant changes only to fall back again. Have you dieted and lost weight only to gain it all back? How about returning to a relationship that you know doesn't work out? Have you made lots of money and lost it all? How many times have you tried to quit smoking? Have you succeeded in making changes and realized your problems have stayed the same? Of course, everyone has at one time or another, but why? Why are these changes temporary? If you are doing everything you think you should be doing, why don't your changes last? There are three reasons:

- You are taking a physical approach to a nonphysical problem.
- You are only using about 10 percent of your power.
- You still need to evolve.

THE NONPHYSICAL APPROACH

The problem with taking a physical approach to your problems is they are not physical. It may appear so on the surface, but the origin of the issue, no matter what, started in your nonphysical mind. For instance, if you believe you are not good enough, it will eventually play out as you not feeling valued or being treated poorly in some way. The outcome is physical, but the belief is nonphysical because it started as a thought, feeling, or emotional experience. Even when trauma happens to the body, it first originates in the mind and is drawn to the body by attraction. Your mind is not physical. Your brain is physical, but your mind is not part of your brain. It is ethereal, nonphysical, and spiritual. You can't access it from your five senses. You access it from your sixth sense. Your feeling senses. That of intuition, insight, trust, faith, inner knowing, etc.

Let's say you have financial problems. Is that a physical problem or a nonphysical problem? The result is physical because you need that money to live on. The origin of the problem is nonphysical, as it started as a thought, emotion, or belief that you carry with you. The problem with a physical approach is it can't penetrate the physical. You may be thinking: what about therapy or psychiatry? Yes. They work and are very effective, but they also have their physical limitations.

When you learn to access the nonphysical, there is no limitation to the depth you can reach, allowing you to release trauma, hurt, pain, struggle, and misinterpreted information stored in your mind.

THE 10/90 PARADIGM

Did you know you only use about 10 percent of your power? Most people think of themselves as a body, but in actuality, you are a complete system consisting of a mind, body, and spirit. The body is just a part of the system, and as long as you only see yourself as that one part, you will only have access to about 10 percent of your whole system.

Here's an example. Think of yourself as an iceberg. Your body, that 10 percent of you that you see and relate to, is above the surface. It is in the physical. The other 90 percent of you, that of your mind and spirit, is below the surface and is ethereal. You focus mainly on your body because that's what you relate to, while the unseen part of you remains untapped.

The average life span is about eighty years. That's a short time in terms of eternity. When you leave the body, your consciousness returns to the spirit and lives on forever, so doesn't it make sense to get to know that part of you now? After all, it is part of your system. You are not a body that becomes a spirit after it dies. You are a spirit with a mind and a body. You are supposed to merge your mind, body, and spirit system to evolve and experience yourself from a higher perspective.

Accessing spirit is the Gift of Divinity given to all of us. This gift of knowledge, wisdom, understanding, peace, and the ability to heal yourself lies within your 90 percent, waiting to be recognized and tapped into. This 90 percent is what you have been waiting for. The next generation of you integrated beyond the limitations of your 10 percent and into your ever-growing, constantly evolving, more significant 90 percent.

YOU HAVE YET TO EVOLVE

You are constantly evolving, but are you doing it consciously? Conscious evolution is mindfulness to the max. It is taking control of your life and intentionally moving yourself forward by tapping into your 90 percent.

Most people still need to do this, but they haven't because they don't want to; they don't know how to. Some people go through life not knowing they are stuck, while others may not realize they can do something about it. How do you know?

Take a minute and think about your life. Do you actively participate? Do you go about life as it happens, or do you pick what you want and go after it? Are you overly concerned about what others think or say about you? Do you worry about making a mistake or looking like a fool? Are you in a bad marriage or relationship because you don't know how to escape it? Are you afraid to be on your own? Ask yourself, am *I stuck in a rut that I can't get out of?*

If you feel stuck, you have yet to evolve. Evolution is freedom. It is the freedom to move forward without fear. As you progress, you know you will always be okay, even if the results don't appear as anticipated. When you haven't evolved, you feel that something is missing in your life or that there should be more to life itself. If you feel an urgency but don't know why, it's time to evolve. You are ready even if you don't know what it means exactly.

Life is changing, and you are changing, too. It is the spiritual puberty that humans are experiencing. It is a call to your nature, asking you to pay attention. It is a return to the wholeness you have been missing for so long. It is the peace within you. It is the trust within you. It is the power within you waiting for you to answer. Are you ready?

VOLUNTARY AND NATURAL EVOLUTION

There are some things in life that you do not have control over. One of those things is natural evolution. Natural evolution is nature taking its course without your conscious participation, such as aging or puberty. You don't consciously think about or decide how many inches you will grow in a year or when you will need to start shaving. It just naturally happens.

On the other hand, mindfulness is voluntary evolution because you are making a conscious effort to make your growth happen. You volunteer to evolve. You make the choices as to what you want and what you feel you need to move forward. You are consciously an active participant in your life, which means you choose to evolve to resolve the situations and circumstances that keep you stuck. Evolution creates resolution, improving your life in every possible way.

EVOLUTION

How do you consciously evolve into a more advanced version of yourself? It's easy. Just follow these three steps:

1. Live your philosophy.
2. Practice empathy.
3. Adjust your frequencies.

Live your philosophy: Do you have a philosophy that you live by? Do you practice the golden rule? I don't know about you, but I found that rule hard to live by. In theory, it is perfect, but when put to the test, it is hard to live up to.

I tried to treat people as I wanted them to treat me, but some people are mean and abusive. When I learned this rule as a child, I was still too mentally and emotionally immature to understand the hardships one might be going through that made them act that way. I tried my best to comprehend, but it didn't alleviate the hurt or pain that I experienced. I felt I had no leg to stand on. If I treat people nicely and they don't respond in kind, now what? I'll have to stop following a philosophy I can't live by and create one I can live by.

Having a philosophy to live by is essential to your identity and well-being because it gives you a solid foundation to build upon. Nothing can knock you off that foundation when you create your philosophy. You know what you are about. You know what you stand for, and as long as you know what you stand for, you don't fall for what you don't believe in. You don't become swayed or influenced into doing what you don't want to do. You become the driver of your life instead of the passenger in someone else's life.

When I started my journey, I sought out all kinds of people from assorted backgrounds to help me find my spiritual path. It took me about seven years of searching to finally figure out that nobody knew more about me than me. They could point me in a direction, but that direction sometimes was based on their beliefs, not mine. That left me feeling rudderless and without guidance, until I finally took my life into my own hands, realizing it was up to me to find out about me. I knew I needed a solid philosophy to stay on course, something I could sink my teeth into and make my own. I realized that everything I had done was in search of me and my relationship with myself, so I created this philosophy. "There is only one relationship, which is the relationship with myself. All other relationships stem from that foundation."

It's all about me. Everything I think, feel, believe, act, and react to is about me. That is something that I can live with every day. I am responsible for everything I think, feel, believe, act, and react to. There is nothing outside of me. It is all inside me, and I live by that truth daily. That is my truth. That is my philosophy. That is my foundation. Nobody or nothing is going to knock me off of that foundation. I know what I am about. I know what I believe. I know what I feel and think at all times. It

44

is my choice what relationship I have with myself and what I choose to have with others. I know that the better my relationship with myself is, the better my relationships are with family, friends, money, career, and health.

When you are creating your philosophy, it has to be about you. It doesn't need to be grandiose, such as "I am the universe's light and shine upon the world." To most people, those are just words. Make it something that has real, intimate meaning to you. Make it simple but profound. One of my students created this philosophy for herself, which is brilliant: "Work hard, play harder." It is simple, to the point, and keeps her on track. Think about your philosophy. Make it about you. Give it meaning and live it daily.

PRACTICE EMPATHY

Empathy is to feel or sympathize with another person. To put yourself in their shoes and see life from their perspective. What is self-empathy? Self-empathy is turning that empathy inward to feel and understand what you are feeling.

You would not believe how many people don't know or are not in touch with how they feel. I know I didn't. I was the "I don't know" person. *What do you want for dinner? I don't know. What do you want to do today? I don't know. What do you want or need to make you happy? I don't know.* I had learned how to not focus or reflect on myself. It was part of my conditioning and, unfortunately, yours too.

Sometimes, you say "I don't know" when you do know. Have you been on a date or out with friends and said "I don't know," because you want to see what they say first? Do you make sure what you want is okay with them before you speak up? Do you hold back a little to ensure you're safe in what you want without appearing pushy or outspoken? Of course, you all have in one way or another.

People often told me to keep my mouth shut or not say anything. It led me to believe that my feelings weren't valid. If my feelings were invalid, it must mean that the person telling me to shut up knows more than me. Therefore, I should listen to them and discard what I want, especially if there are any signs that they disagree with me. After all, I didn't want anyone to get mad at me. I didn't want to be bothersome or a troublemaker, so I let myself believe that what they wanted was better than what I wanted, and I just got on with life. Easy enough? Right? Wrong. What happens when you give into the wants of others at your expense? You lose yourself. You lose who you are, what you want, and what you stand for. You lose your identity and individuality. That is, if that you had those in the first place.

If you don't know yourself, you live for what others want. Living this way can make you angry, resentful, and other harmful things that take you further from yourself. It can also leave you feeling empty and unfulfilled because you give to those around you without getting your share back in return. It may not be that you want much, but you do need to communicate your wants, needs, and desires in a way that is heard, acknowledged, and respected.

Knowing how you feel is vital to your life. You can't live your life if you ride along in someone else's life. You have to steer your ship mindfully. Knowing how you feel and what you want allows you to determine what works and does not. It gives you the critical information necessary to understand what and how to change it. It seems simple enough, but how do you change your feelings? You change them by adjusting your frequencies.

ADJUST YOUR FREQUENCIES

Have you noticed how some people get under your skin for no apparent reason, while others you instantly take to? Have you walked into a place and not liked the way it felt? Did it give you an eerie feeling or creep you out somehow? The reason is you are picking up on the frequencies of that person or place. Frequencies are signals that you can't see. They are a form of unspoken language or communication that guides you toward or away from what is in your best interest.

Frequencies are the energies or vibes you give out and receive. For instance, you have heard of someone having a good or bad vibe, right? It's the same thing, only you want to know what frequencies or vibes you are giving out so you can change them if they don't help you. If you have heard of the law of attraction, you know that like attracts like. If you are resonating at frequencies that are low in vibration or damaging, such as hatred and unfairness, that is what you attract to you. On the flip side, if you are vibrating at more positive frequencies, such as love and peace, that is what you will attract to you. Here's an example: I've never met anyone who felt worthy and good about themselves and had chronic money issues, but I have met people who have had money and lost it because they didn't feel worthy or deserving of keeping it.

The great inventor Nikola Tesla said, "If you want to know the secrets of the universe, think in terms of energy, frequency, and vibration." If you want to know the secrets of your universe, you have to think of yourself in terms of energy, frequency, and vibration. Think beyond your physical self or five senses and into your nonphysical or sixth sense.

Everything in existence is energy, and it all has vibrations and frequencies. You are the same way. You are energy and carry unique frequencies that vibrate at different rates. You want to find what frequencies you attract through self-empathy and change them into frequencies that are good for you by practicing the Mindkeeping technology.

It's like tuning your car radio up or down to get the desired signal. Have you been stuck in between stations or on a weak signal that is just irritating? Your energy is the same way. If your frequency is off, it can be annoying and make you miserable. So many people walk around angry, anxious, irritated, frustrated, depressed, and so on because they don't realize they tune into the wrong frequencies. Once you recognize what to change and learn how to change it, everything in your life gets better because your system is in harmony with the energy you desire to have.

For instance, if you desire happiness but attract disappointment, you will miss the mark and not find that happiness. It's not because you don't deserve it or because of something you did that you have to pay for. It is simply because your system hasn't adjusted to the higher frequencies that allow you to experience that happiness.

Your mind is more than your thoughts. Your mind is a system like a computer or cell phone. When you know how your system works, you have the power to change it by expanding past the frequencies that limit you and into the more advanced higher frequencies that make your life better.

THE UNIVERSAL LAWS OF NATURE

Spirit (lumen) is our nature, and human is our experience. By nature, you are energy. Everything in the universe is energy vibrating at different frequencies. Higher frequencies, such as love or kindness, resonate at a higher frequency and make you feel good. Lower frequencies, such as resentment or fear, resonate at a lower frequency and make you feel bad.

Here's a scenario. Let's say you are a diehard football fan watching your favorite team. You are psyched and enthusiastic because it's the playoffs, and your team expects to win. The game starts. Your team receives the punt on the twenty-yard line and runs it back eighty yards for a touchdown. The crowd roars. You cheer triumphantly, vibrating at a high frequency because you are happy and excited that they are winning.

Your team kicks the ball to the opponents, and they fumble. Here comes your special team's guy, ready to pounce. He recovers the football, and you cheer again. You feel nothing can go wrong. You are excited, happy, and feeling good because you are resonating at a high frequency. High and happy---that's you until the fourth quarter of the game.

Your team is winning by twenty-one points. You feel that they are at the finish line, and you are ready for the post-tailgate celebration. There are five minutes left to play. Your team has the ball and goes for a pass. It bounces off the receiver's chest and into the arms of the defensive player, who runs it into the endzone for a touchdown. You feel annoyed but are still up fourteen points, so you can live with that.

The opponents' kick-off and your special teams' player drops the ball. The opposing team picks it up and runs it into the end zone for another touchdown. How are you feeling now? Not as high and happy as before, but still okay. Doubt starts to creep in. The players that were heroes a few minutes ago are beginning to become zeros to you now. You may even call them names futilely to make them play better. Your energy is beginning to change. Your frequencies are changing, and you can do nothing about it because you either don't know how or aren't aware of it.

Two minutes left to go in the game. The score is 21-14 in your team's favor. The opposing team kicks off; your receiver gets the ball and runs it to the fifty-yard line. You cheer up. Things are looking up, and your frequencies are rising. It feels good until the next play when they fumble again. The opposing team recovers, scores, and goes for the two-point conversion to win the game. You feel your heart sink. You yell at your team for losing. Your frequencies have entirely shifted from feeling good to feeling bad. These changes happen every day in life. You go from having highs to lows without realizing that you can change how you feel by simply changing your mind.

Chapter 4

Perception Is Everything

THE GOD PERCEPTION

I think most people believe in God or a higher power. Be it Christian, Muslim, Judaism, or whatnot. Many of you learned that this power exists and everyone and everything is part of it. Do you believe you have the same traits and attributes as a child of God? Do you have the potential to be everything, be everywhere, and be omnipotent? It seems so, but do you believe that it is possible? No, because it would change your beliefs about yourself and your world.

What if God, as you perceive it to be, is different than you thought? If you put yourself in a different scenario or a simulation, would you or could you experience your relationship with God differently? My experience is YES. I experienced a difference when I changed my thoughts and beliefs about God with what I felt and experienced.

Just for this moment, forget what you know about God. I'm not debating the Bible's texts or the great books written for humankind to follow; I am simply giving you a new twist on an old subject: you and God.

Let's pretend that the story you know has a plot twist. What if the real story was more futuristic, like a sci-fi movie? Let's imagine that human is not a species but a machine, similar to Alexa. What if you were a machine and God was the source of power and information? What if you could input the information given to you by this God power and grow exponentially? The more you grow, the more intelligence you gain, giving you powers and abilities beyond your current capabilities.

Wouldn't that make you more god-like?

Here's another scenario. Think of God as the source of all the information and power in the universe, like an infinite iCloud and library of knowledge of everything and everyone in creation. This source is so vast that you can only grasp a tiny fragment like a speck of sand. Yet within this speck is more information than you could absorb because you can't handle it as you are now. What do you do? Do you do nothing knowing that you have the potential to be more than you are now, or do you find a new way to expand your intelligence from the most reliable, loving, and powerful source to make your life better?

Lastly, imagine you are a machine like a cell phone. Instead of having a serial number, you have a Social Security number. Your race and gender determine the make and model of your machine. Your power comes from a power source you plug into and an energy force that turns you on and animates you. Once you are charged up and turned on, what happens next? Nothing. You sit idle until you input what you want it to do. Your phone doesn't text, call, or download by itself. Neither do you.

The mind, body, and spirit connect like your phone connection. Your spirit is the energy source that you plug into. Your mind is the energy force that turns you on, and your body is what inputs the information into the system. You don't consider your cell phone separate even though it has independent parts. You see it as a whole system. It is one system with individual parts, but they all work together. If the battery is dead, it doesn't work. If you break the casing and crush the components, it doesn't work; if you can't plug it in to get power, it doesn't work, period. It is a system that works in unison and in harmony with itself.

Your system can only work correctly with you. You are the critical element in making everything happen. As you see yourself as a system, you understand how your system operates. You know your system is physical and psychological, but did you know it is empathic, too? Empathy is what you feel, but I am referring to self-empathy. Self-empathy is the communication between what your spirit wants and your soul needs. It helps you recognize how to discern situations and circumstances and prompts you to change and upgrade as needed. Like a notification on your cell phone, empathy alerts you to change. Without this connection, you can't do much, but with this connection, there isn't much you can't do.

Changing your perception of God changes your life by strengthening your relationship with your inner self. This understanding allows you to become the programmer, analyst, and repair tech within your system with the ability to change the hurts and pains that keep you stuck in the same loops and patterns. It's simple. It's like downloading an app. Once connected, you determine what you want or need and drop it into your system. It may not happen overnight, but it will happen.

Do you need confidence? Download it. Do you want a career change? Download it. Do you want healthier relationships? Download it. You are at the helm of your system. Some requests take longer than others, but if you continue to practice and strengthen your connections, you will surely be open to a whole new level of you.

It is simple. It is easy. It is a different way of interacting with yourself that allows you to live beyond the physical limitations and into the spirit, which soothes the soul.

HARMONY OR CONFLICT?

Does expanding your mind conflict with your spiritual or religious beliefs? Not at all. Developing your mind enhances your spirituality and strengthens your character, making you stronger and more able to communicate with this part of you. It also increases your faith and trust, allowing the best of you to shine.

Spirit is an experiential force of nature. Each of us experiences it differently; there may be some similarities, but each individual has their unique path and set of circumstances. Mindkeeping is the tool to help you find that path and experience spirit as part of you, not apart from you. Physical and nonphysical, human and lumen, are two sides of the same coin. Each of you is born with this system intact. Now, it is time to integrate that system so you can make choices that propel you toward your spirit instead of away from it.

Are you in harmony with your life or in conflict? Most say it's a harmonic relationship, while others say it's conflicting. Conflict sneaks up. It is so tricky that you probably don't even realize it. If you feel this way, you might be in conflict.

Let's say that you have a good life. For that, you are grateful, but on the flip side, you yearn for more. You don't know what you want more of, but you know you are missing something. You feel fortunate yet unfulfilled and guilty and wrong about feeling that way. You are grateful for your blessings and upset with yourself for wanting or needing more. You try to ignore your feelings, leading to frustration, resentment, and blahness. You go through the motions of life without really enjoying it. Why? Because you forgot who you are or never had the opportunity to explore who you are because life and circumstances didn't give you a chance. You feel like you live for others and that your wants, needs, and desires are secondary or don't matter. You are the passenger in your life instead of the driver. You sit on the bench but only participate in the game once life throws you a curveball, and you have no choice but to pick up the pieces.

How do you get out of this "whatever" state of mind? What do you have to do to avoid this altogether? It doesn't take much. All you have to do is see yourself in a new light.

ACT LIKE A SPIRIT

You have to be spirit to know spirituality. You don't need an intermediary to tell you how you should feel. It is up to you to decide because only you can experience your inner self. It all boils down to you. It is a choice. Do you want to become Spiritual, or do you want to keep on pretending you are less than you are?

If you don't know yourself, you don't know your spirit, and if you don't know your spirit, you can't be your best self. They are the same—a different part of the whole system. If you only see yourself as part of the system, you unknowingly pretend to be less than you are. That's what humans do: pretend. You pretend to be less than you are, which ultimately doesn't help or solve your problems.

Pretending to be "just human" is painful. It creates hurt, pain, suffering, and confusion. It discounts you and takes you away from who you are, so it only makes sense to upgrade your interaction in this world.

To be Spiritual, you must change your thoughts by interpreting spirit from your standpoint. If you are a spirit, you control your life and are the master of your destiny. As a spirit, you are loving and merciful. So, of course, you will create a good life. You will create a life that is powerful and kind. You will create a life that is happy for you and one that will positively impact, change, and influence the world around you.

As a spirit, you don't ask yourself what Jesus would do. You ask yourself, *what do I do* because you are the most qualified to answer that question. As a spirit, you don't compare yourself to someone else. After all, what would spirit compare itself to? As a spirit, you are the top dog. You don't need permission or validation from anyone else. You're spirit! You know what is best for you and what makes you happy.

Being spirit means you don't have to keep reliving the past because that goes nowhere. If you are supposed to go back, you would have eyes in the back of your head. You can also alleviate suffering because, of course, to be spirit means to be complete, which, in turn, makes you whole (holy). As a spirit, you understand that talking about being Spiritual doesn't make you Spiritual. Living it allows you to expand your mind by consciously knowing there is more to learn and more to be. You know happiness is a way of life, not a fleeting moment. As a spirit, you know that you are to be happy and that defining what that means is up to you. Spirit knows happiness trumps struggle, and struggle is only a direction back to happiness.

Being spirit means you know the body is temporary and just an experience. You know you are so much more than what you had previously believed. You accept the greatness that is you, full of love, compassion, forgiveness, and encouragement, while embracing the flaws that come with being human too.

Being spiritual is not for the weary. It takes strength, tenacity, and dedication mixed with tears, doubt, and frustration. It is not an easy lifestyle, but it will be your life's most fulfilling and rewarding experience once achieved.

Chapter 5

The Next Generation

WHAT IS YOUR LUMEN MIND?

The lumen mind is an upgraded version of the human mind. Some refer to it as the Christ consciousness or the Second Coming of Christ. This second coming does not mean that Jesus returns to save us; it means that the energy and mind of Christ return to us so that we can save ourselves.

Think of it as your sixth sense. This sixth sense is the glue that connects you as an individual to your higher source of power. Although lumen has always existed, most could not access it because they didn't understand it. Now that there is technology to mirror what we are capable of, it is comprehendible and attainable.

You use your lumen mind every day without realizing it. It happens every time you go beyond your five senses. You tap into your lumen mind when you go beyond taste, touch, smell, sight, and hearing. You are tapping in if you trust your gut or instinctual nature. Visualization is another way of tapping in, as is insight, intuition, wisdom, and synchronicity.

Your feelings are the gateway to your lumen mind. Learning to trust them will allow you to develop these senses more deeply. As your higher senses develop, you rely on them more frequently and integrate them into your conscious mind.

Your lumen mind is constantly working with your human mind. Here's an example. How many times have you thought of someone and they call you? You might say, *I was thinking about you. How weird.* It's not strange. It is you tapping into your lumen mind. Have you had a precognitive dream? Did you feel like something was going to happen before it did? How about that feeling that you know something good is coming, or you feel excited but you don't know why? All of these are indicators of your sixth sense and lumen mind.

You will notice more synchronicities, such as looking at the clock, which is 11:11, 3:33, 4:44, or some other significant number. You may start to wake up at a particular time in the middle of the night. You may experience stranger-than-usual dreams or feel that you are traveling in your dreams. You may begin to know things but discount your feelings by thinking it is too weird to be true.

All these are signs that you are expanding, and the more you trust these anomalies, the more experiences you bring to you. For instance, my brother was in a fender bender the other day. He does not practice spirituality or necessarily believe in anything he can't see, but he did say, "It was strange; I had a premonition about it before it happened." He said, "I had this vision and heard metal colliding like a car crash. I just brushed it away and didn't think about it again."

He had unknowingly tapped into the sixth sense that warned him to be careful or more mindful of his actions. However, he didn't heed the warning.

He turned left across a three-lane road; two lanes had stopped, and the third lane looked clear. It wasn't. As he turned past the first two lanes, a truck came out of nowhere and hit him.

Everyone was okay. No one was hurt, and my brother's car and the truck were moderately damaged. All's well that ends well, but if he had trusted what he saw, he may have been able to avoid that problem altogether.

That goes for everything in life. When you feel something is not right in your gut, it's not right! Trust that. When you don't like someone, pay attention to your feelings. If you know you should not do something and do it anyway, learn to trust yourself instead of regretting it later.

Your higher senses help and provide for you in many ways. Here are a few examples of how living from your lumen mind can help you in your everyday life.

Are you in sales? Your lumen mind enhances your intuition, giving you the insight and information to know what your clients need even if they can't communicate it. In other words, you can hear what they are not saying and find solutions to their objections. Enhanced senses close the deal, and isn't that what you want: to close the deal and give your customers what they want?

Lumen mind enhances your empathy. Empathy is a fantastic tool if you are a team leader or even a parent trying to motivate their child. Understanding what others are feeling or where they are coming from gives you the knowledge to inspire them. When you are on the same wavelength, communication becomes much easier because you know how to connect with them on a higher level and give them the support needed to help them achieve their success.

The lumen mind turns raw potential into reality by giving you the power and ability to make it happen. What good is knowing what you want if you don't have the power to make it happen? Fine-tuning your higher senses gives you the creativity to create opportunities that didn't exist before.

Lumen mind helps you turn old patterns, beliefs, and habits into new perspectives and insights by removing the debris within your cellular memory. Using these higher senses allows you to see beyond what you believe to be accurate and into the truth. When you can see the whole story instead of a part of the story, the information becomes clear, and there is no need or desire to hold onto old hurts, pains, traumas, or habits that keep you from moving forward and being happy.

Living from your lumen mind gets you out of your head and into your instinct. There isn't anyone I know who couldn't benefit from this, especially if you are having trouble letting go of the past or suffering from overanalyzing. Athletes and competitors like it because it helps to keep them in a state of mind that enhances their performance. When you get in your head, everything becomes more laborious, which could lead to fatigue and doubt.

You certainly don't need that if you are trying to put your best foot forward. Enhancing your higher senses expands your instinctual nature, which helps you to naturally anticipate the next move, be it yours or your opponent's. Lumen consciousness gives you greater confidence and trust in your abilities, taking you out of any negative headspace.

Trusting your senses helps you stay happy and healthy. When you are happy, you are naturally healthier. It also reduces anxiety and stress by helping you recognize when your energy is out of balance. It also guides you in repairing it, creating balance within your mind, body, and spirit system, thus potentially saving you and your employer thousands of dollars on health care and medical bills.

Living in your lumen mind increases your intelligence, wisdom, understanding, and the ability to heal yourself and those around you by giving you access to information and insight that you previously didn't have access to.

HUMAN OR LUMEN?

The difference between being human and being lumen is determined by what consciousness you are connecting to. A human being relates to the physical human consciousness. A lumen being relates to the nonphysical consciousness and is spiritually fluid, meaning it can move back and forth from material consciousness to spiritual consciousness at will.

A lumen being can move beyond physical consciousness. Although in the body, it is free to roam to different and higher parts of the mind, giving it access to knowledge and information that it can't access from the human consciousness. One is not better than the other; it is just a different experience of itself. A lumen being is not more spiritual than a human but is more in touch with its spiritual nature. A lumen realizes it is spirit in human form instead of human only.

HEADS OR TAILS?

Making decisions can be challenging. I don't know about you, but I have flipped a coin or two so I wouldn't have to choose. It's usually over something insignificant, like do I want Chinese or Italian for dinner. The bottom line is the choice is always mine. That's a beautiful gift we all have—the power to choose. You can choose who you love, decide where you work, and choose who you hang out with. These are all your choices, even though, at times, it feels as if you have no choice.

The great thing about it is that you have a choice and the power and authority to choose what is best for you no matter what, when, where, how, or why. Choice also gives you complete and total control over how you use your mind. It sounds impossible based on what you have learned, but you are the wizard behind the curtain. You are creating your life's joy and drama by your choices. You can choose what you want or don't want or let someone else decide that for you. One option will make your life better, and the other will not.

So, what are the choices? What possibilities do you have to choose from? How do you know you are making the right choices? Have you made a decision only to second-guess yourself? What if you could make a decision and have complete confidence that it is the right choice for you? How would that feel?

What would life be like if you knew you were always on the right track? Impossible. It's not, and here is why.

Imagine that your mind is like a coin. One side is heads; the other is tails. You are in the middle choosing which side of the coin you want to connect to. Each choice has two distinct possibilities and outcomes. One side of the coin is human and physical. The other side of the coin is lumen and nonphysical. Both belong to you, and you have complete authority over your choice. Each side works differently. You already know how to use the "tails," or human, side of your mind. Now it's time to learn the "heads," or lumen, side of your mind. Remember, they are part of the same coin, and you can and will use them interchangeably.

The more you connect with your lumen mind, the better you feel because it is in sync with your spirit and not with the role you temporarily play in the body. It may sound challenging, but it's not. It is effortless. All you have to do is make a choice.

Which side of the coin (your mind) do you choose to connect to?

They both exist in every given moment and situation. Once you know how to choose, you can be an active participant in your life instead of an inactive observer waiting for someone or something to tell you what to do next.

You are the keeper and authority of your mind. No one and nothing has the right or power to control you in any way unless you allow it to. Pay attention to your choices, as what you choose is what you create. If you choose fear, fear will control you. If you choose faith, faith will guide you. One side leads to limitation, and the other side leads to evolution. It is up to you to choose heads or tails (lumen or human). Both sides are yours to create whatever situation or circumstance you desire.

When you choose the human side, you don't always realize that your actions or lack of actions create your reality. You can mindlessly create unhappiness, disappointment, limitation, fear, worry, insecurity, struggle, and even disease. I am not saying that your life will be miserable, but that choice can put you in a position of not understanding why things don't work out positively for you. It can prompt you to keep repeating the same mistakes or have you blaming others for your situations and circumstances while feeling powerless to do anything about it. You find yourself surviving instead of thriving, and all that can be changed by simply making a different choice.

If you choose the lumen side of the coin, you consciously become an active participant in your life. As an active participant, you know you are creating your own life, so you mindfully create loving, positive, uplifting, prosperous, kind, fun, happy, and blessed situations.

Human/Physical	Your Choice	Lumen/Nonphysical

Both sides of the coin represent your mind. How do you differentiate between the two? The easiest way to remember is that everything human is outside of you. It is physical, like your body, your car, your house. All of these things are physical. You experience them externally.

Everything lumen is internal, or within you. Like your feelings, your ideas, your intuition. You experience them within you, not outside of you.

Both sides are part of the whole, but you predominantly use the human side because you have yet to access your lumen side mindfully. The distinct differences between the human mind and the lumen mind are:

HUMAN MIND – EXTERNAL

The human mind is external - experienced as outside of you.

The human mind consists of matter. It is material.

The human mind is mindless. It is not consciously awake.

The human mind is three-dimensional.

The human mind uses five primary senses.

The human mind is divided and dual. Yes/no, good/bad, etc.

The human mind is thought-driven. Mentally motivated.

The human mind goes along in life, a passenger.

The human mind is limited.

LUMEN MIND - INTERNAL

The lumen mind is internal - experienced as inside of you.

The lumen mind consists of light. It is ethereal.

The lumen mind is mindful. It is consciously awake and aware.

The lumen mind is multi-dimensional.

The lumen mind is multi-sensory: sixth and higher senses.

The lumen mind is unified. All is one.

The lumen mind is emotional, feeling-motivated.

The lumen mind drives life.

The lumen mind is unlimited.

You will see a significant difference between the two. The human is what you know about you, and the lumen is what you remember and integrate within you.

The most important thing to remember is "Everything inside of you projects outside of you." " In other words, your MBS system (mind/body/spirit) is like a giant projector, and earth is the screen. Whatever you are feeling inside, you project out into the world. Nothing exists outside of you unless it first exists within you. Think about your life. If you have inner turmoil, you will have outer turmoil. If you have inner peace, you will have outer peace. The calmer you are on the inside, the more peaceful your life is on the outside.

Again, everything human and physical is external and perceived as outside and separate from you. For instance, notice how these phrases project the issue or problem away from you. *They made me do it. Nobody treats me right. She won't listen. Work is the problem.* Do you see how the blame or responsibility gets put on someone or something outside of you?

Everything that is lumen is internal. It comes from within you and is yours. You take responsibility for what is going on in your life, giving you the power to change it. These phrases have you taking ownership of what you feel inside. For instance, *I let that happen to me. I choose to have better relationships. How can I express myself in a way that I feel heard? I don't like my job; it's time to find something different.* Do you see that you are taking responsibility for participating in whatever just happened?

You must grasp this concept to change your life and evolve. Taking responsibility for your deeds, actions, and choices makes you a consciously active participant in your life. The more you participate, the more you grow, and your life changes naturally for the better. Here are a few more examples.

Nobody treats me right. Who is *nobody*? Is *nobody* one person or everyone you know? Why are you allowing them to treat you this way? How do you want to be treated? Do you feel you deserve better? No one but you has the authority to make those decisions.

Most people don't know the answers to these questions. It's not because they don't want to. It is that they hadn't thought to ask themselves the questions. You have learned to blame others for your lot in life, but when you take your life into your own hands, life changes because you change. You no longer rely on the information outside of you; you rely on the information inside you. The internal perspective allows you to find the truth about your feelings and wants and take back what is rightfully yours. You don't have to be stuck. You have the power to change, but you can't do it from the outside. You have to do it from the inside because the lumen mind makes the changes last.

Another example of internal or external is the statement: *They don't listen to me.* As soon as you say "they," you look outside yourself. You are blaming them, whoever they are, for not listening to you. When I am working with clients, and they make that statement, nine times out of ten, the problem is the client needs to convey the message. It happens over and over again. The client is upset for not being heard, but when asked if they expressed their feelings to that person, they say no. They feel that whoever should know what they want, or they don't want to deal with the drama, so they say nothing.

There is also the occasional yes to that answer, but it always ends with, I am so tired of yelling. I know from my own experience that yelling doesn't work. No one wants to be yelled at, and most people ignore it. Even though you are expressing yourself, it is not what you say but how you say it. You know the expression "You catch more flies with honey…"?

Not all people are intuitive. They need you to be direct with what you want, or your expectations. People are reasonable for the most part, and if they know that something is bothering you and you communicate that to them, they will make any reasonable adjustments. If it is someone who cares about you and your well-being, they will want to listen because you are important to them.

If you are afraid to speak up, that is an entirely different issue. What scares you about speaking up? Are you afraid the other person will get mad at you? Do you feel that what you say doesn't matter? Do you not want to cause trouble? Are you afraid of sounding foolish?

If you answer yes to most of these questions, that's okay. Many people feel this way. You've been conditioned not to speak up, but that doesn't mean that what you say is unimportant. It is. It is important to you because that's the way you feel. You can't blame others for how you feel. You have to take control of that yourself. The best way to take control is to ask yourself, *Is this choice human or lumen? Does it take me closer to myself or further away?* The choice is always yours, but you'll get much further if you work from the inside out.

INNIE OR OUTIE?

Do you remember being a kid and comparing belly buttons? "Hey, do you have an innie or an outie?" It's funny how you remember things that have no significance and sometimes forget the things that do. That is the nature of life. You remember what you want, as you want when you want. Life is easier this way, in the sound bites and snippets you choose to remember. But what does that have to do with being an innie or outie? It doesn't really. It reminded me of the importance of understanding you from an internal versus external perspective.

The human perspective of life is external, and the lumen perspective of life is internal. Everything that happens on the inside gets projected on the outside. You view life as a movie projected onto the screen of the world without realizing that you are that movie's writer, director, and actor. You think you are observing that movie instead of creating it, but as you begin to understand that you are the writer, the movie changes. You want to be more involved. You want to write new scenes and change the direction. You have a vested interest, which makes you more responsible and accountable for what you are creating. Another way of looking at it is that life is happening to you, or you are creating what is happening.

When you think of things as external, you blame others or circumstances for your life or where you are. That's not to say that things don't happen. Of course, they do. That is life, but to what degree and why it happens is up to you. It is all up to you because you are the only one who can change your life. If you blame others, life is fruitless and will never change, but when you take responsibility, everything in your life changes for the better. Example: I have a client who came to me because she said (in her words) her husband is a "selfish asshole." She claims he took *everything* from her and only thinks about himself. Is it true? Yes, if you look at it from the external perspective. He did take liberties in their marriage, and it was not an equal partnership, but who is responsible for that? Him or her? She is because it is her life.

To see it externally, you would believe that she is right and he is a jerk, but what is her responsibility in the relationship? As I have said before, a relationship is a relay of information back and forth. If there is only one person, there is no relationship, so what is her responsibility? Externally, not that much. She determined that he was an ass and it was best for her to leave him, which she did. She left him but didn't leave behind the anger, hurt, frustration, financial fallout, and everything else that came with that experience. That's not going. That's holding onto or possibly transferring it to the next partner that comes along. When you live externally, this is what happens. You don't resolve the problems. You hold on to them or transfer them, as you haven't yet realized the wisdom of having them in the first place.

To view this situation internally, she understands that although she still thinks he is an ass, she is at peace with herself and doesn't need to lash out at him. She understands that her role and participation in this relationship was to learn to stand up for herself and experience more equitable experiences. It was also for her to see and understand that she has value not because of him but because of her, and she no longer needs to pay for love. When I say pay for love, I mean it in the sense that you don't feel good enough, so you think you have to supplement yourself in some form, be it in extra time, attention, money, support, or in a way that gives more to the relationship than you receive in return.

By seeing herself from the inside out, she could see what she was creating and why she was creating it. She could let go of the anger and hurt that kept her stuck and move forward, freely giving herself the supplement she had given others. Although she lived most of her life as an outie, it didn't take her long to turn it all around. She is now happy, healthy, vibrant, and renewed because she decided to live as an innie instead of an outie.

Chapter 6

Becoming a Mindkeeper

BE LAZY; DO IT RIGHT THE FIRST TIME

When I was nineteen, a boss told me, "Be lazy; do it right the first time." This statement was so profound that I made it a rule of life. I like laziness. I want to avoid repeatedly doing something because I was hasty or too immature to take the time to do it right the first time. That makes no sense to me. That is not to say that I do everything in my life with due diligence, but I make sure I am lazy about the important things.

If it is true that we reincarnate until we learn the lessons needed to ascend this earthly existence, why not be lazy and do it right the first time? Why on earth (no pun intended) would I want to do the same things repeatedly? Why would I want to feel heartache or disappointment over and over again? I want to be lazy, find the cause of these issues, and transcend them pronto! I want to change those negative feelings to something positive. I want to live a happy life, not a stressful one. I want to be lazy and move through these uncomfortable energies as quickly and as efficiently as possible. I want to raise my consciousness and awaken my life by recognizing and understanding that I created it. Everything that happens to me is by my own doing. Whether I like it or not, I did this and am the only one who can change it, just as you are the only one who can change it for you.

It may seem ridiculous to blame ourselves for the heartache, pain, and struggle, but doesn't it make sense? How else do we learn to get out of our way? After all, isn't that how we teach our children? We let them fall until they know how to walk and stand on two feet. The lessons they learn mold them into who they are. Some people understand this, and their experiences are more manageable, and others don't get it at all, instead cursing God or others for their shortcomings. It can be hard to swallow at first, but once understood, it will catapult you further than you could have imagined.

Here's an example: I have been practicing healing for over thirty years. I even created a holistic health group called Life Plan Alternatives in the mid-'90s. It consisted of a group of like-minded practitioners, doctors, and other professionals to inform the general public of alternative ways to improve their lives and health. I rented a location for us to practice and created a speaking series presented weekly at Border's Books, Barnes and Noble, Whole Foods, and anywhere else willing to have us. It was free information for the public, and we were glad to share our knowledge.

Everything was great. The presentations were successful, and everyone was picking up business. Everyone but me, that is. I had provided the platform, the location, and the advertising, but what was I getting in return? Nothing, I thought. I started to feel resentful. I was hurt and disappointed that the group didn't support me as I felt they should or as I had helped them. In time, it all came to crumble. Everything I created fell apart. The individuals went on. In some cases, they were stronger than when they had started, and I was crushed and devasted. My heart felt ripped out of me.

So, what's the problem? I was being lazy, but not in a good way, instead of being lazy and doing it right the first time. I was just being lazy. I was being lazy about myself. I was promoting the group and not promoting myself. I thought that by osmosis, the public would see who I am and what I had created and reward me for it.

Wow! Talk about illusions of grandeur. How could the public acknowledge me if I don't tell them who I am and what I do? I didn't do that and was mad at everyone else for it. Suppose I had been lazy and done it right the first time. I would have given myself the time, focus, support, encouragement, and platform I gave others. It wasn't their fault. If someone asked me if I wanted to tell a receptive audience about my business, all I had to do was show up. I would have said, "Hell yeah, sign me up."

No matter what challenges you have in life, face them head-on. Be lazy and do it right the first time. Don't procrastinate, and do your best not to live in denial. Denial only prolongs the discomfort and agony that you put yourself through. Be lazy. Streamline the process and enjoy the extra time you have to give to yourself.

KEEP YOUR MIND

You have learned NOT to keep your mind but to tend to the will, feelings, attitudes, and desires of others at your expense. That may sound like a bold or selfish statement, but it is not. The more you live for others, the less you know yourself, and if you don't know yourself, you have nothing to offer others that is yours. You can play back and mimic what they want, but you are not necessarily doing what you want because you are still determining what you want. When you don't know what you want, you become the passenger in someone else's life, eventually leading to boredom, frustration, resentment, and unhappiness.

What would you think if someone came into your house and cleaned it unexpectedly? At first, you may think that's great, but what if that someone moved all your things? What if your spoons were now in your underwear drawer, and your underwear was in the garage? Besides being confused and frustrated, you might feel violated too. That's your stuff; nobody should be moving your things unless you tell them to.

When you hire a cleaner, they don't move your things. They may organize or rearrange with your permission, but it is up to you how you want your house cleaned and your things arranged.

The same goes for your money. You certainly wouldn't give strangers or even family members access to your accounts. If you did, you would not control what goes in or out of that account.

Your mind is the same way. You control what goes in and what comes out at all times, or at least that is how it should be. Unfortunately, you have learned differently. You have learned to listen to others at your own expense. You have learned that giving is better than receiving, which is not equitable and does not create balance in your life. You have learned that your thoughts and feelings don't matter if they hurt another's feelings. You have known not to make waves or cause a scene that might upset or embarrass your family or friends.

When you are the keeper of your mind, you know what you want. You know what you are about. You know what you stand for. You know what makes you happy and how to attain it. By keeping your mind, you know that you must give yourself what you need first so you have the resources to help others, too. You must have the resources to avoid burning out and becoming mentally, emotionally, or physically bankrupt.

Mindkeeping gives you the foundation to stand for your beliefs without fear that you will be coerced or swayed by someone else's dreams or desires. It allows you to be your own person with rules, defining who you are and how you project yourself into this world. It takes your deepest wounds and makes them your greatest strengths. Your mind is infinite, and so is your ability to stretch it. How far can you or do you want to go?

SPIRITUAL PUBERTY

Now is the time in your life that I call spiritual puberty. It is when you no longer want to be who you were and are moving into the next and better version of yourself. It is a growing pain and the discomfort that comes with growth, like a seed of a flower through the dirt. It is the realization that there is more to life than what you are currently experiencing and the desire to find what that is.

You all have a time in your life or even a couple of times when you no longer feel like you fit in. You feel like you are changing or things around you are changing, and you are no longer content. What used to be okay with you is no longer okay. For example, you have a friend for a long time, and you get along great until one day, they start getting on your nerves out of the blue. You may not know why, but something feels off. Then you begin to see things about them you didn't see before. You may start to recognize that you give more in this friendship than they do or you don't enjoy being around them as much as you used to.

Another example is you want more. You start to think about what life means or ask yourself, *Is this all there is to my life?* You want more but are still trying to figure out where to find it or feel guilty for wanting it.

Most people that I work with are between forty and sixty-five years old. They have their careers in place with some expendable time and income; however, they feel guilty or wrong for wanting more. It's not that they think they don't deserve it; they feel bad for not being happy with what they already have. They have good lives. They have a good family and career. They have nice things but still feel that something is missing. They feel torn between being grateful for what they have and feeling guilty for wanting more.

It's not more things they want. It's more meaning they want, and that is perfectly okay. When you get to a point where you have many things, such as a family, house, career, cars, vacations, and more but still don't feel content, it's time to look at you. The things don't fulfill you. You fulfill you. Your mind, body, and spirit connection gives you the depth and meaning you seek, and finding it comes with growth and discomfort. It's puberty in a different form. It is you growing beyond the physical and more into the spiritual. It is like growing in places you haven't grown before and finding a new depth and maturity about you. It is the kind of puberty that takes you from being human to being lumen. *Human* being physical and *lumen* being light within your physical body.

Some feel no urgency, but for others, there is great urgency. Suddenly, you feel as if the clock is ticking away. You don't know why but feel you have more to do. You feel as if time is running out, but you don't know what it is running out from. It isn't that you think you are going to die; it is the feeling that you have more living to do.

To an empathically sensitive person, what once felt like a pea under your mattress now feels like a full-sized boulder. You can't ignore it even if you want to. Spiritual puberty knocks on your door with a feather, and if you don't open it, it comes in with a battering ram. It is your wake-up call to look at yourself and start to evolve. It is one of the reasons you came here, if not the main reason. To grow, develop, and understand yourself from the perspective of spirit. It is you calling you. Are you ready to answer the call?

WHAT ABOUT ME?

I've been hearing some statements about how nobody cares. The truth is everybody cares; they care more about themselves than you, though. That's okay, as that is the way it should be. You are the keeper of your mind and your own life. It is not up to the government to care about you. It is not up to your employer to care about you. It's not someone else's responsibility to care about you. It is your responsibility to care about yourself. When you genuinely care about yourself, you naturally care about others and the world around you.

I know times are tough. Watching other people's agenda affect our lives is frustrating and aggravating, but that doesn't take away our right and power to care about ourselves. In this time of chaos, I challenge you to ask yourself, *What about me do I care about most? What about me do I value and respect? What about me can I build on to make myself and the world around me a better place? Who is willing to join the challenge?*

ONLY YOU CAN DEFINE YOU

What are you about? What makes you unique? What makes you different? Do you define yourself, or does your past define you? Did your parents or siblings define you? She's the sensitive one, or she's the bossy one. What about your work? He's a hard worker, or he's lazy. Does your environment define you? She's a Jersey girl. He's a redneck. The only thing that matters is that you define yourself.

You are not your past. You are not what your parents, siblings, friends, or spouse say you are. You are what you choose to be. It is up to you to decide who you are, what you want, and what you want the world to know about you. It is up to you to choose your partners and friends; it is not up to them to choose you. You are an individual. Find out what that means for you, and live in that space. Do you need help figuring out where to start? Start with how you see yourself. Do you like what you see? Do you like the person you are and where you're at in life? If not, what don't you like? Is it the way you look, feel, think, or act? Is it something you can change easily, or do you need help? Are you evaluating yourself accurately or seeing yourself through a convoluted lens?

I give my students a questionnaire to help them to get in touch with their perception of themselves. One of the questions is: How do you see yourself? Do you see yourself in your true light, or do you judge yourself by what you think you should be? Are you seeing the positives and being truthful about the negatives, or are the hurts, pains, and struggles of the past impacting your perception?

Do you take one step forward and two steps back by seeing a positive trait and canceling it with a negative? Can you accept the perfection that is you with all of its' flaws? After all, isn't that what you are: flawed perfection? The imperfections give you character, empathy, wisdom, and compassion. Be open to the idea that you are already perfect in your messed-up, imperfect world. Give yourself the chance to see yourself as happy, kind, caring, self-sufficient, warm, creative, capable, intelligent, and so on. Allow others to see the real you instead of the façade. Show them your true character, not the illusion hiding behind the façade.

How do you see yourself, and how do you want to be seen? These are two of the most powerful statements you will ever answer. These are the questions that help define you. Only you can see yourself positively and project what you want into the world. I choose to see myself as kind, wise, intelligent, compassionate, resourceful, blessed, strong, spirit in a human body. I project myself into the world as a spiritual leader, author, healer, influencer, evolutionist, and lumen being in this human experience with wisdom beyond my physical consciousness. I decide who I am and how I project myself into the world. Not you, not my past, and not anybody or anything else. I have been down that road before of letting others define me, leading to disappointment. So, I ask you again, what defines you?

BEING A MINDKEEPER

What does it take to be a Mindkeeper? What do you have to do?

When I started, I hated everything about meditation and quieting my mind. I found it tedious and frustrating. If you told me to relax, my mind would go into automatic overdrive. Quieting my mind made me irritable. It was as if I felt forced to do something unnatural. I couldn't sit properly either. I cannot sit cross-legged. My body doesn't go that way. I've tried to, but it made me cranky because it hurt. You may be thinking, no pain, no gain, right? No. If there is pain, I'm not doing it. Lastly, add on the breathing component. Breathe in two, three, four; hold it, breathe out two, three, four. OMG! I'm going out of my mind. Are you telling me to relax, think of nothing, sit in pain, and breathe in a way that I have to catch my breath? Not for me. I could not grasp it. It didn't make sense to me. I had to find an easier way. So, I did.

Mindkeeping is a practice that doesn't require you to quiet your mind, sit like a pretzel, or breathe a certain way. Those are all add-ons; if you choose to incorporate them later in your practice, so be it. For now, the only thing you have to do is follow this one rule:

Be accountable for everything you think, feel, believe, act, and react to.

THE MINDSET

Do you have a mindset? Do you steer yourself one way or the other at any given time? Do you psyche yourself up to diet or for a big game or performance? Mindkeepers have a mindset. That mindset is "I am responsible for everything I think, feel, believe, act, and react to." It is up to me and only me to define myself, and this includes:

My identity: Who am I-/how do I want to be perceived? How I perceive myself.

My creativity: What am I creating? Do I like my life/-my character/my experiences?

My expression: Am I saying what I want to say? Am I owning that my voice is important? Am I being heard and acknowledged?

My body: Am I balancing the energies of my body with my mind and spirit? Am I accessing the hidden information stored in the cells that helps me awaken, evolve, and heal?

My consciousness: Which system am I working from, physical/

human or nonphysical/lumen? Am I consciously recognizing, merging, and expanding?

Past or present: Am I living in the past, or am I living in the present moment?

IDENTITY

Why is your identity so important? It is because it is how you see yourself and project yourself into the world. Your identity can slip away if you aren't paying attention to that. It happens all the time, and, in some cases, you have no real identity. You become everything you think you should be or learned to be instead of deciding for yourself what that identity looks like.

An example is when asked what you want or what makes you happy and you need help answering that question based on you alone. You may say happiness is having good friends and family, but taking everything external out of the mix leaves you with you. What specifically makes you happy? Do you have a hobby? Do you have a passion? What did you enjoy when you were a child? What might you like to explore? What makes you uniquely you?

CREATIVITY

What are you creating in your life? Do you like your life? Do you like yourself and the people around you? Is your life constantly a struggle, or is it peaceful with a little bump in the road here and there? We all know life has ups and downs, but do you have more downs than ups? You are creating your life, so you must be mindful of what you create. If you don't like what you have made, you can create something better. The only catch is knowing what you are creating so you can change it. Life is the canvas, and you have the pencil. Feel free to draw outside the lines and use the eraser to create your masterpiece.

EXPRESSION

Expressing yourself can be a challenge. I am old school. I come from a generation where children should be seen and not heard. Can you believe it was like that at one time? Yikes! No wonder we are screwed up.

Your expression is your most powerful tool. You can create and be anything you want if you can be heard and acknowledged. The problem is that most people need to speak up or learn how to use their voice. Many feel that what they say is unimportant or think others should know what they want.

Others don't know what you want. If they did, they would most likely listen and react accordingly. The clients who tell me that nobody listens to or respects them are usually the clients who don't speak up. They believe their spouses, children, co-workers, and family should know what they want. It doesn't work that way. People are not mind readers. They only see what you want if you kindly and respectfully tell them. I say *kind* and *respectful* because screaming and yelling don't work. Nobody wants to be screamed and yelled at. If you yell at me, I shut down and tune you out. Most people do the same thing. If you are in a cycle of screaming, yelling, crying, and complaining, I can assure you that does not work long-term. You may get your way temporarily, but things will go back to how they were because whomever you are directing that complaint to has already tuned you out or is only in agreement to calm you down. Knowing what you want to say and feeling confident enough to say it will get your voice heard, acknowledged, and respected.

BODY

Most of you think of your body as your identity. You are a person inside of a body. You all know that caring for our bodies is in our best interest. You learn to eat right, exercise, drink water, and get enough sleep, but what if you looked at your body as a house for your mind that reflects your spirit? A storage system of skills, talents, thoughts, memories, ideas, and so on waiting to be awakened? Everything you could ever want or need lies within your body's cells; all you have to do is access it. Think of it like exercise for your body, but instead of working from the outside, you are working from the inside out. It is a physical exercise in a different form to balance and build your cells to access the hidden information within your system.

CONSCIOUSNESS

Are you mindful, intentionally paying attention to what you think, feel, believe, act, and react to, or are you mindless? *Mindless* does not mean you don't have a mind. It means you are not paying attention to your mind. You allow life to happen to you instead of you consciously creating it.

Do you remember me saying you are two sides of the same coin? When you are mindful in a practical way, you choose which side of the coin you want to operate from. Are you being human or lumen? The choice is always yours and only yours to make. When you make choices that empower, you expand. When you make choices that disempower, you contract. Expansion helps you to access your hidden talents. Contraction keeps them secret.

PAST OR PRESENT

Are you living in the past, or are you being present? Being present gives you the power to change your life. Living in the past or blaming others does not. When you refer to a past event, you are no longer present to make the change. For instance, blaming someone or something for what they did to you takes you out of the present moment and emphasizes the other person. If you are being present, the emphasis is on how you feel and what you want to change or do about it. When you give that other person or situation power, you are no longer present to change it. Mindkeeping emphasizes you and gives you the accountability you need to stay in the present.

TAKING ACTION

Now that you know what it takes to be a Mindkeeper, it is time for you to put it into action. Do you remember the three core principles of Mindkeeping?

1. Create a philosophy.
2. Practice empathy.
3. Adjust your frequencies.

Here is where you create your philosophy. Your philosophy is the foundation that you build upon. When you have a philosophy you can believe in and live by daily, you will always have that foundation to rely on when things in your life get complicated.

A great example is an article I read the other day. A firefighter from Florida miraculously escaped death because of his philosophy. He was filming an instructional video in a lake near Tampa when a twelve-foot alligator suddenly attacked him. An overhead drone caught the whole thing on camera. The firefighter did not see the alligator until it chomped down on his skull. The injuries to his head were extensive, leaving him with a crooked face and more surgeries in the future. Fortunately, because of his training and philosophy of life, he instinctively fought off the alligator and could call for help. When asked what kept him going through this bloody ordeal, he responded, "with steely determination and my philosophy for life"; "Sometimes in life, our plans change. And when they do, we just have to swim harder than we've ever swum before!"

Thankfully, he is okay, but he may not have made it out of that situation if he did not have his philosophy to fall back on. Your philosophy is so important that it becomes more than words. It becomes instinct.

What is a statement or phrase that supports you that you can live by every day? What's your philosophy?

CHAPTER 7

HEAL – Human, Evolving, and Lumen Mind

"Y ou think of yourself as a body and your mind as your thoughts, but you are more than that. You are a whole (holistic) system."

The human mind is the physical state that keeps us believing that we are bodies with a spirit instead of spirits in a body. This chapter will show you the differences between the human, the evolving, and the lumen mind and the importance of evolution.

You think of yourself as your thoughts instead of a whole system.

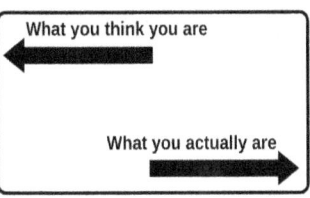

What you think you are

What you actually are

WHY EVOLVE?

To live, thrive, have fun, and enjoy life without the baggage. Evolving is fun. It's like going on a treasure hunt; only the treasure you seek is you. You are an explorer on the journey of your life. You find a clue, and you solve a problem. You keep digging, and you find a new skill or talent. You dig even deeper and find a more incredible version of yourself by returning to your natural state of mind. As I have said before, you are only in your body briefly. It is a costume you wear and a role you play. You return to your spirit when the play ends. You have forgotten about this part of you yet yearn for it, not consciously but in a way that makes your soul feel restless and unfulfilled. It is that feeling that something is missing from your life. It is believing there is more to life but being unable to put your finger on it. It is wanting to help others but not knowing how or in what capacity.

THE HUMAN MIND

Perception is everything. I believe that wholeheartedly. People believe what they perceive regardless of the facts. Politics is an excellent example of that. Ask a Republican what they believe, and they will defend it because they know they are right. Ask a Democrat what they believe, and they will defend it because they know they are correct too. It isn't the message itself but how the individual perceives the message.

The majority of the world believes in a higher power or God. The names may differ from religion to religion, but the reverence and respect are the same. Most of you can agree with that, but did you know how you perceive this higher power is what may cause you to feel stuck? You have learned to perceive God as apart from you instead of a part of you. Even though you know it exists within you, you don't perceive yourself as the same or equal to it. You see it as outside of you or need an intermediary to intercede. Even though you know and believe there is a connection, you still understand it as more of a concept than a reality. In other words, you may understand it intellectually, but you don't live it emotionally.

Your human mind believes that you are separate from or less than God because you only see yourself as a body or conceptualize yourself as the thoughts in your head.

Some may even feel fearful of God or intimidated, believing that they are not worthy of or deserving of being one with that source.

From this perspective, no matter how hard you try, you will always feel separate from this energy source.

HIGHER AND LOWER PERSPECTIVE

In the diagram below, you see two intersecting circles. The top circle is your spirit, and the bottom ring is your body. Within the two intersecting circles is a connection. It is not a significant connection, but it is connected nonetheless. That connection represents your human consciousness. You know there is a connection to your spirit, but you don't feel as consciously connected to it as your body.

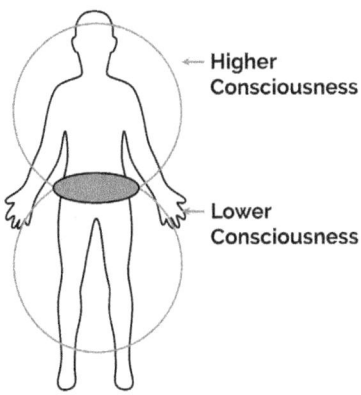

In the diagram:
- ← Higher Consciousness
- ← Lower Consciousness

Below is a different perspective that breaks down the attributes and characteristics of your human mind

Human Mind

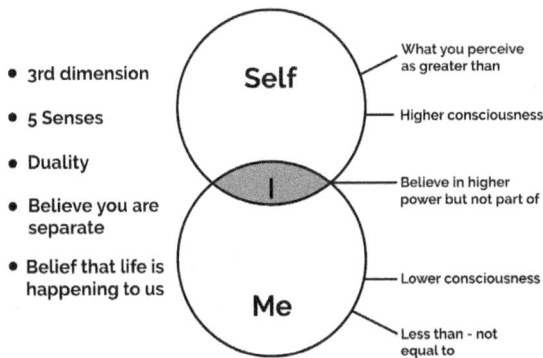

- 3rd dimension
- 5 Senses
- Duality
- Believe you are separate
- Belief that life is happening to us

Self

I

Me

- What you perceive as greater than
- Higher consciousness
- Believe in higher power but not part of
- Lower consciousness
- Less than - not equal to

- The human mind is three-dimensional with the capacity to be multidimensional.
- It is limited by the physical five senses: - taste, touch, smell, sight, hearing.
- It thinks in terms of duality: yes/no, good/bad, right/wrong, heaven/earth.
- You believe your mind, body, and spirit to be separate entities.
- You believe that life happens to you instead of creating your own life.

THE EVOLVING MIND

The evolving mind begins to experience itself differently. As the higher and lower consciousness integrates, it creates a greater sense of itself. It is where mindfulness and mindlessness meet to create a balance between the systems.

Evolving Mind

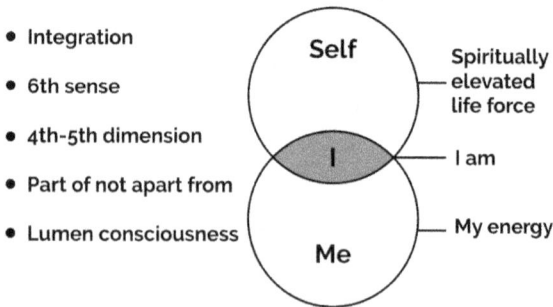

As the intersection expands, so does your consciousness. You begin to experience your higher senses and dimensions and start feeling a part of instead of apart from. You connect to yourself as a whole unit where mind, body, and spirit (*me, myself,* and *I*) become significant to you and your evolution.

Some people feel uncertain about this space because they are no longer who they were and not yet who they are becoming. Think of it as reinventing yourself. You will move through evolution with minimal discomfort as long as you know that growth is what you are experiencing.

THE LUMEN MIND

The lumen mind is a unified consciousness.

Your lumen mind frees you from the illusion that you have to be anything but what you already are, and that is the I AM or I of God. The I of God is your unique sense and expression of you. It is your mind awakened and your spirit personified in physical form.

What happens when you are in your lumen mind? You identify with your spiritual nature as much as or more than your human nature. Your intelligence grows, as evidenced by aha moments and the realization that things that used to bother you don't bother you anymore.

You become consciously aware of your thoughts, feelings, and actions and how they affect you either positively or negatively, giving you the power to let go of things you couldn't or wouldn't let go of in the past.

The trust, confidence, and belief in yourself improve, as does your self-esteem and image. You stop judging yourself and replace it with compassion and acceptance. You are more at peace with yourself, creating more stability in the people and situations around you.

Overall, you have more information to work with, which sparks more inspiration and creativity and increases intuition, wisdom, knowledge, and understanding.

You also become a direct link to God, no longer needing an intermediary to reach the source. Everything in your life improves simultaneously; however, remember that even when you have access to your lumen mind, you are still in the human experience. You will continue to make mistakes and be vulnerable to the human condition. However, you can navigate it faster with more mental and emotional options and clarity to rectify the situation.

Lumen Mind

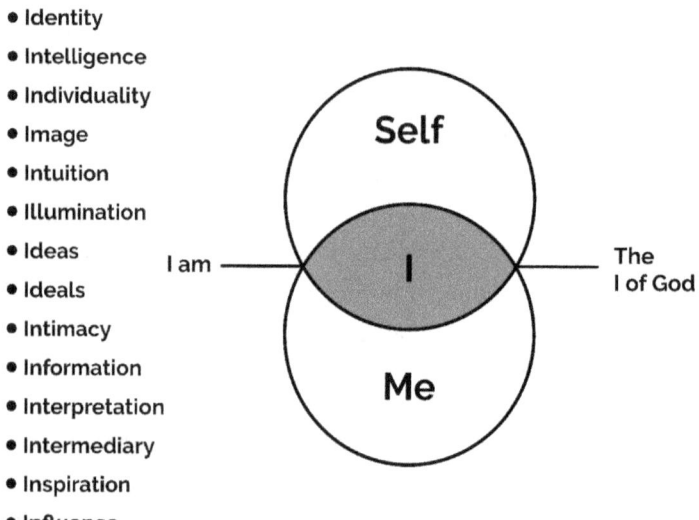

- Identity
- Intelligence
- Individuality
- Image
- Intuition
- Illumination
- Ideas
- Ideals
- Intimacy
- Information
- Interpretation
- Intermediary
- Inspiration
- Influence

I am — I — The I of God

Self

I

Me

ME, (MY)SELF AND I AS MIND, BODY, AND SPIRIT

You will notice that I have inserted *me, self,* and *I* into the circles. For some, this is an easier way to understand how consciousness relates to them individually. I have also created an acronym to help identify how you interact with each part.

M.E.: My energy or my ego. What and how you identify your possessions? Everything you refer to as *me, my,* or *mine,* such as *my thoughts, feelings, beliefs,* etc. *My* is the part of you stored in the lower consciousness.

(My) **S.E.L.F.:** - Spiritually elevated life force. SELF is your higher mind—your spirit. It is the nonphysical lumen consciousness connected to universal wisdom.

I: - (I AM.) *I am* is the integration of M.E. and S.E.L.F. within the body and consciously living between human and lumen consciousness. You may know this as Christ's consciousness, the *I AM,* and what I call the "I of God." What you refer to as *I am, I will,* and *I shall* are all part of this integrated consciousness.

FEELING THE DIFFERENCE

You can feel the difference between *me*, *myself*, and *I* by just saying them out loud. When you say *me* or *my*, as in *my mind*, *my life*, *my things*, and so on, it has a lower vibration than when you say *I am*. Try it.

Say out loud *my life*, *my story*, *my money*. Add *my* before anything, and allow yourself to experience how that feels in your body. You can feel it pushing inward near your solar plexus.

Now, say *I* or *I am*. As in *I know*, *I will*, *I shall*, *I don't want it*. Can you feel the difference? The *I* is more forceful. It is more commanding. It has more conviction and can be felt in your chest as if you were thumping your chest. For instance, when you know something for sure, you know. You have that conviction and authority over it. My friend Linda and I have a joke about this. When she or I say something the other agrees with, we say, "I know!!!!!!!!" (overemphasized) We are sure of what we know to be accurate, and it also makes us laugh. I know this is a silly exercise, but you will be surprised when you try it. My students always get a kick out of it, which helps them start recognizing how the different frequencies feel within their bodies.

Spirit	My self
Mind	I
Body	Me

SUMMARY

You know that the human mind thinks it is separate from, the evolving mind understands the concept it is part of, and the lumen mind experiences itself as part of and belonging to.

The lumen mind knows its connection to everything, be it God, the universe, itself, and others. It experiences itself as equal parts of *me*, *myself*, and *I*. When *me* and *myself* merge, it opens the door to the "I of God." or the *I AM*—the individual expression of you in its highest form channeled through your mind and body. The *I AM* is your unique fingerprint manifested into the physical world. It is you realizing and experiencing that you are more than you thought. You are, in essence, a God in your own right. I am not saying that you are God in the sense of being the all-mighty, all-knowing creator of existence. You become the I of God when your mind understands its individuality within and is part of the greater whole. Think of it as being a leaf on a mighty oak tree.

As the leaf at the bottom of the tree, you may not realize that anything exists beyond the branch you connect to. You feel separated from your source until the time comes when you can expand your existence into the greater reality that you are part of a more extensive system. You are no longer a leaf but a part of the tree, an integral part of the whole system consisting of all the other leaves, branches, trunk, roots, earth, world, universe, and so on.

The lumen mind is the conscious understanding of you as a system connected to a more extensive system and supported in all you do or want to do. It is you as a divine personal computer with your individualized apps and search engines. When you know how your mind system works, you move beyond your ego, rooted in the human mind, into the self in the lumen mind to consciously create from the inside out. What is so great about this? When the ego recognizes itself as spirit, miracles happen!

THE STOOL

My family has a saying that we are the stool, referring to a three-legged seat, as our family has three siblings. Each of us represents a leg.

We know that the stool only works with all three of us. It takes each of us to do our part to support the other. Your mind is the same way. It takes all of the elements to support it. Sometimes, one leg will be stronger or weaker than the other, but the other two legs make up the difference, ensuring that integrity and balance are maintained. Consider *me*, *myself*, and *I* as the stool's three legs.

Each leg is essential; although you may think one is more important than the other, it is not. Your spirit is crucial but not more important than your body or mind. Mind, body, spirit, or, if you'd rather say, *me*, *myself*, and *I* are all siblings in the same family. Each plays its part to ensure that the whole is solid and stable. They constantly communicate and are allies, always striving for what is in their highest and best interest.

CHAPTER 8

The Lumen System

"It is time to raise your consciousness and change because the old vibration is not working anymore."

Most people think of their minds as thoughts, but your mind is more than that. It is a system. Similar to how your body is a system. You know your body has a heart, lungs, brain, muscles, tissues, and so on, but you don't think about it. You instinctively trust that they will do what they are supposed to do. Your mind is the same way. It, too, has different parts. I want you to be aware of them but not dwell on them, as it will not change the effectiveness of your practice.

The first thing in understanding your mind system is knowing it is energy. Do you remember the Nikola Tesla quote?" If you want to know the secrets of the universe, think in terms of energy, frequency, and vibration." If you want to know the secrets to your universe, think about it as energy, frequency, and vibration. Remember, everything in the universe is energy, and all energy has frequencies and vibrations. As energy, you are flexible and fluid, not fixed and solid. When you can determine what frequencies you are emitting, you know what frequencies cause havoc on your system, giving you the knowledge to adjust them.

The way to find your frequencies is to look inward. Do you remember the two sides of the coin? Human (external) versus lumen (internal)? You will be working on the internal system, meaning that everything you think, feel, believe, act, and react to is yours to fix. Everything outside of you is only a projection of what is inside you. It starts internally within your mind. In then out. Remember that, and you will have no problem.

The other thing to keep in mind is how you process information. Do you process by thinking or feeling? A little of both, perhaps. However, you are likely more thought-driven unless you are empathic or sensitive. Empaths are natural feelers, which can be confusing in a thought-driven world. This confusion can lead an empath down a dark road if they don't know how their system works. I will address that later in the book. For now, it is all about what system you are using. Are you thinking or feeling?

Your mind is energy in motion. It is the emotions that drive the mind, not the thoughts. Think of your mind like a car. The feelings are the gas, and the thoughts are the steering wheel. You can steer all you want, but without fuel or power, you sit there. Emotions move energy; they change vibration and frequencies. Moving energy is why getting in touch with how you feel is so important.

Additionally, your thoughts can play tricks on you, but your feelings don't. Have you seen a mirage or an optical illusion? You could swear that you saw something that wasn't there.

Have you walked into a room where a conversation was taking place, and suddenly, the conversation stopped? What was your reaction? *They must be talking about me.* Then, you rack your brain to determine what they could say about you or why. You become uncomfortable and start letting your thoughts run wild when, all along, they weren't talking about you at all. They may have been discussing something personal, or the conversation could have been over.

Your mind will make things up to appease you, but your feelings don't lie. You may not always want to acknowledge or accept what you feel, but what you feel belongs to you and you alone. It is your direct roadmap to what is in or out of balance within your system.

What you feel does not have to make sense, nor does it need to be justified. You feel the way you do for a reason: telling you what needs adjusting to make your mind and life happy.

THE PARTS OF THE MIND

Your mind has parts just like your body does. You don't dwell on these body parts; you know they exist and trust they work unless you are in pain or have a problem. I want you to think of your mind in the same way.

I will explain each part to you for clarification. You don't need to know this information to practice successfully. If, at some time, you want to delve deeper into each piece, by all means, do so, but for now, everything you need is already built into the practice for your mind to evolve simultaneously.

The five parts of your mind system
- Breath
- Chakras
- Subtle bodies
- Grids of consciousness
- You

BREATH

Breath is life. If you are not breathing, you are not living. I can't emphasize the importance of taking deep breaths throughout the day. Hold your breath. It's good for you, but use good judgment as you don't want to pass out. Holding your breath and letting it out slowly helps you on so many levels. Deep breaths change your mood, slow you down, release anger, tension, and much more. Notice I am not telling you to follow your breath. It is not necessary for this practice. Just remember to breathe throughout the day. It is vital to the well-being of your mind.

CHAKRAS: ENERGY CENTERS OF THE BODY

Chakras are invisible energy centers within your body that are not physical but etheric. There are seven major chakras. They are root, sacral, solar plexus, heart, throat, third eye, and crown. The root is the first chakra at the base of the spine, moving upward toward the head. A different color represents each chakra and resonates at a different frequency. The colors are red, orange, yellow, green, blue, indigo, and violet from root to crown. Each chakra is associated with a different organ of the body and characteristics of the mind. I am only providing the basic information on the chakras to familiarize you with the parts of the mind. Plenty of information is available if you want to search deeper; however, this is all you need to know to have a successful practice.

Side view – Chakras – conical-shaped energy centers within the body

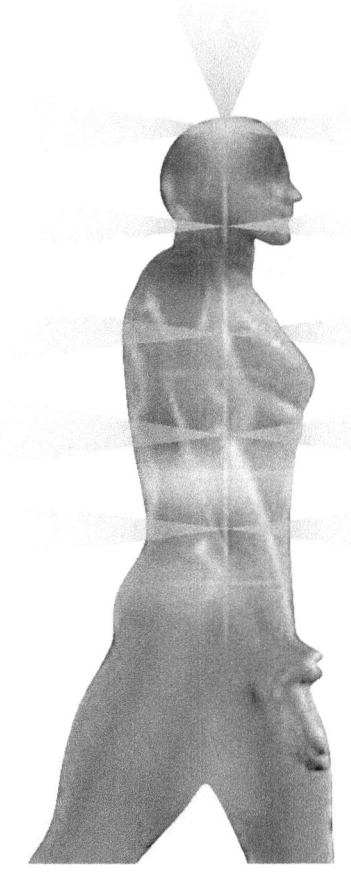

Front view

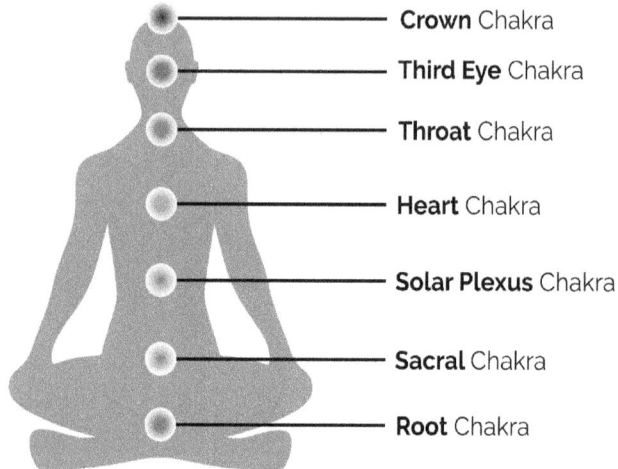

- Crown Chakra
- Third Eye Chakra
- Throat Chakra
- Heart Chakra
- Solar Plexus Chakra
- Sacral Chakra
- Root Chakra

- **Red — Root —** Security, Life force, Foundation
- **Orange — Sacral —** Creativity, expression, manifestation
- **Yellow — Solar Plexus —** self-worth, identity, will
- **Green — Midpoint — Heart —** Love, compassion, relationships
- **Blue — Throat —** truth, personal expression, self-worth
- **Indigo — 3rd eye -** vision, insight, problem solving, seeing from a higher perspective
- **Violet — Crown —** Divine purpose, enlightenment, healing

**Lumen heart — Located between the heart and throat chakra also known as the sacred of high heart

Fun Fact: Why are we called humans? Because we have a hue, or aura, of color around us.

SUBTLE BODIES

Subtle bodies are invisible energy fields that extend beyond your physical body. Have you ever heard anyone talk about auras? *I like your energy*, or *she has a good aura about her*? That is what you are sensing. Seven subtle bodies directly overlay your physical body. The seven subtle bodies are your light, or nonphysical body. Each has a unique color, and each vibrates at a different frequency. The seven subtle bodies extend from the closest to the body to the farthest away. They are the etheric body, emotional body, mental body, astral body, etheric template two, celestial body, and causal body. From closest to farthest, the color scheme is the same as the chakras. That is red, orange, yellow, green, blue, indigo, and violet. Each body serves a specific purpose, as described in the outline and the diagrams below.

As with the chakras, there is plenty of information about the subtle bodies available if you want to learn more about them. However, for this practice, it is not necessary.

Etheric Body: Closest to the physical body, extending a few inches from you. Life force and connection between the physical body and the other subtle bodies.

Emotional Body: About 1-3 inches away from your body, this body holds the emotions, feelings, and emotional functions.

Mental Body: Extends 3-8 inches from the body. It contains your ideas, cognitive processes, thoughts, and beliefs.

Astral Body: Connection between the lower and higher bodies, astral projection, out-of-body experience, quantum leaping (leaping into alternate realities)

Etheric Template 2 Body: Blueprint of the physical on a higher level and parallel universe

Celestial Body: Connects to the divine. Awareness and alignment to the universe

Causal Body: Some call the soul. Knowledge of lower bodies and the Divine (the All-Knowing)

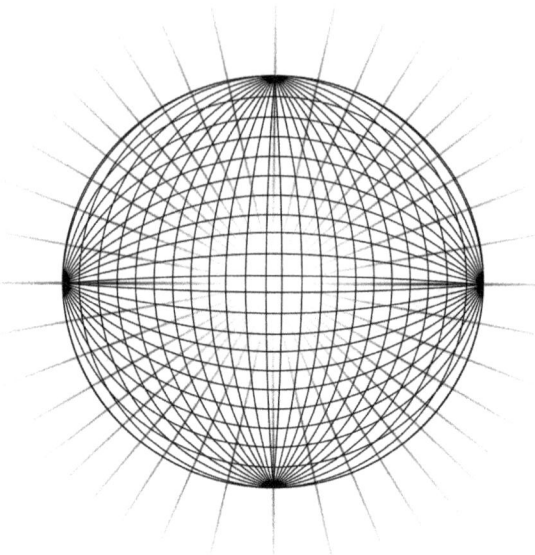

THE GRIDS

The grid is the network that connects your mind to different dimensions of experience and understanding. Think of it as an information highway. You have roads and highways to travel physically; this is how you travel mentally. Below is an explanation of what they do, but again, don't dwell. Just know it exists.

- A grid is a dimension or experience of consciousness.
- Frequency is how you change your consciousness.
- Empathy is how you change your frequency.

Dimensions of your consciousness vibrate at different frequencies. You might have a happy thought that resonates with a high frequency or feel emotionally disappointed, and you resonate at a lower frequency. Your thoughts and emotions are constantly flowing through these grids, as are your frequencies.

If you want to change, you must change the frequencies within your mind. In other words, if you're going to change your consciousness, you have to change the frequency of that consciousness.

Sometimes, you will get stuck in a dimension that is painful or has you making the same mistakes repeatedly. That's like having your TV or radio tuned in between stations. It's frustrating and irritating, but the program becomes clear when you adjust the tuner to a better frequency. Since you are not a radio or TV, you must tune yourself into the best frequencies. The way to do this is through empathy. Knowing how you feel gives you the power to change the frequencies within you.

YOU

Nothing happens without you. It is you who breathes life into you. It is your energy centers/chakras that connect to the source. It is your subtle bodies that send and receive frequencies. It is your choice how you travel the grids. You are the essential ingredient. Without you, nothing happens, and if you don't participate, you become stuck and outdated.

Equate yourself to this. Imagine you buy a new cell phone. What is the first thing you do? You take it out of the box and plug it in. Once charged, you turn it on, creating a force or action that animates it. So, you are all charged up and ready to go; now what? Nothing! Nothing will happen until you make it happen. You have to input what you want for the action to occur. It doesn't happen automatically. You are the one that makes it happen. You are the one that sets the course of action.

PROGRAMMER, ANALYST, & REPAIR TECH

Your mind is a system similar to a phone or computer. A cell phone is constantly evolving and upgraded by technology. Your mind is similar to that system but without intentional updates because no one can program that information for you. It is up to you to become the programmer, analyst, and repair tech of your system to upgrade it to a better network or consciousness.

You are the programmer because you decide what you want and don't want within your system. For instance, if you want peace and happiness, you must program your system for peace and happiness. You do that by analyzing the information within your system that interferes with your desired program. With this new information, you can repair the program by replacing it with a more advanced and efficient program that is in harmony with your desires instead of in conflict with them.

You are in charge. You are the one who chooses what you want and how you want it. You are the chief cook and bottle washer with complete carte blanche and authority over your mind. You can stay where you are or upgrade your system, but remember to treat your mind as good or better than you do your things.

CHAPTER 9

Human Technology

The definition of technology is taking what is factual and existing and improving on it practically and consistently. The only difference is that now you are applying this idea to you. Modern technology improves your life, but human technology improves you.

Modern technology is getting ahead of us, and it is time to catch up. After all, why shouldn't you have the same intelligence or chance of intelligence as Alexa? The only difference between you and it is emotional intelligence. You can gain intelligence, but information without emotional maturity leads to disaster and disappointment. Look at the world. Need I say more? If the world evolved emotionally, there would be an understanding that there is unity in all things.

Emotions are the fuel behind your actions, so it is essential to make sure that you know what you are doing emotionally. For instance, have you ever flown off the handle for no apparent reason? Afterward, you might have thought, *what was that all about?* You may have even regretted it, but what caused that reaction in the first place? Your emotions did because your emotions were managing you instead of you controlling your emotions. When I say *control your emotions*, I don't mean suppress them; I mean know them. Be mindful of how you feel, not mindless, because your emotions are much more significant than you think. For some, feeling may be a new concept, as you believe showing emotion is a sign of weakness.

You might have heard statements such as *suck it up, don't be a baby*, or *you are too sensitive* that make you feel wrong about your reactions; however, those statements are not factual. You can never be too sensitive when it comes to how you feel. Your feelings are the barometer by which you measure what is in harmony or out of sync with you. If you are empathic, that is another thing I will cover later in the book.

Emotions motivate you and direct your life. It is the emotional energy that fuels the fires of change. Emotions can move you forward or backward. When you are mindful of how you feel, you direct those feelings in the direction you want your life to go. When you are mindless about it, it can seem as if life happens to you or you become a victim. That's not to say you have a terrible life. It just isn't your life. It is not the life you've created for yourself. It is the life that you have. The life you create makes you the driver of your life; otherwise, you can feel like a passenger in everyone else's life.

HUMAN TECHNOLOGY

Human technology improves your life by taking you beyond your five senses and into your higher senses. Think of it like a computer. You use cloud technology and virtualization to access almost any information you want to use in your daily life. Human technology is similar; instead of using machines to make it happen, *you* make it happen. You are the technology, expanding your mind by accessing new information that was previously unavailable.

Anybody can access this information through self-reflection, self-empathy, and alchemy. I call this technology SOAR because it is what you need to Set up, Organize, Analyze, and Repair your mind. You follow the technology and are on your way to a better and easier life.

S-: Setup

O-: Organize

A-: Analyze

R-: Repair your mind

When you learn to SOAR, your life takes off in a new and positive direction, giving you the freedom to live the life you create instead of the life you have. Learning to SOAR is all you need to do to change your mind and life.

The process is simple. You find the problem you want to change through self-reflection. You analyze it through self-empathy and repair it using a simple form of alchemy. It is straightforward and can be done anywhere, at any time, with measurable results. I will break down each step to give you a better understanding. At first, it may seem challenging because you are interacting with yourself in a new way, but once you get used to it, the rest is easy. Follow the questions, answer them as best you can, then repair them.

SETUP

The setup is the most essential step in the whole practice. If you only did this and nothing else, you would be okay, but do not omit this part, as it is the foundation of the practice. The setup does so many things on so many levels for you. It creates the lumen body. The lumen body is an exact spiritual overlay of your human body. Although it already exists and doesn't technically need to be made, I have added it because it is an integral part of the connection process. The more you connect, the greater the bond between your mind, body, and spirit. The setup also creates greater focus and protection throughout your day and practice.

The setup makes you an active participant in your life instead of the passenger in someone else's life because you are the one who is consciously and intentionally making everything happen. Lastly, the setup helps you to become more spiritually fluid, meaning you can move in and out of dimensions more easily. Spiritual fluidity may sound scary, but it's not; it is similar to getting an idea. When you get an idea, you temporarily move from the physical (human) third dimension into a nonphysical (lumen) fourth and higher dimension, where that idea lies dormant. You do it all the time. You don't think of it in terms of traveling or jumping dimensions. When spiritually fluid, you do it more consciously to get the information you want or need.

For instance, when working with clients, I need to know their storylines to help them overcome their problems. By being spiritually fluid,

I can tap into the information required that is nonphysical and apply it in the physical. You can do this too. It is a helpful tool that allows you and the other party to create win-win situations for almost any problem or circumstance.

Being spiritually fluid does not mean you are a mind reader. It means you can gather information from the nonphysical and apply it to the physical. Spiritually fluidity helps you in all aspects of your life, for yourself, family, career, or community.

BEFORE YOU START

Before you start, find a comfortable place to practice. Sit in a chair, lie on your bed, do whatever is comfortable for you. It does not matter what position you are in; what matters is that you are comfy. I never sit cross-legged. My legs don't go that way. To some, it is natural; to me, it's not. I discovered years ago that if I am uncomfortable, I will not be as effective in my practice, so I make myself comfortable. I don't sit like a pretzel or breathe in any particular way. I am proof that you don't need that to make this work. There are too many other distractions in life, so let's take being uncomfortable and focusing on what you should do out of the mix.

The setup is easy once you get used to it. I am breaking it down into four parts to help you understand why you are doing it and the importance of each step. I will streamline the process for you a little later.

- Breath
- Invocation
- Connection
- Intention

BREATH

You start with your breath. Remember, breath is life. If you aren't breathing, you aren't living. Breathing is essential to your well-being. Take deep breaths throughout the day, especially before your practice. Clear the air, sort of speak. Cleanse your mind and release unnecessary tension stored within the body. Breathing relaxes you and puts you in a state to receive the necessary information that is coming in for you. Please note I did not say follow your breath or breathe a certain way. You don't need that for this practice. Remember to breathe deeply and more often and integrate that into your day.

INVOCATION

Invocation is vital because it assures you draw in the best and highest energy. Think of it like a stranger at your door. Just because someone is at your door doesn't mean opening it is a good idea or safe. You want to be sure that the energy you are letting into your mind is benevolent and for your highest good. Not all energy is kind, and it certainly doesn't have the same filter you do. It does not consider itself good or bad; it just exists. It is best to determine what energy you want. Do you want the energy you think of as light or the energy you feel is dark? Make sure you know what is at your door by requesting the presence of light be with you.

Invoking is personal. Do it in the way that feels right to you. Call upon the energies and entities that make you feel safe and comforted according to your belief system. For me, an invocation goes like this. "I now call to all of my angels, guides, teachers, mother, father, God, friends, and family of light to come forth at this time of holy communion, and I give thanks. Amen." It doesn't have to be complicated. You can say, "God be with me now. Thank you, amen." If you noticed, in both instances, I said *now*. The reason is I want it now, not later, not tomorrow. *Now* is in the present. I am in the present; therefore, I am requesting help now. I always give thanks, too. Gratitude goes a long way, as it heightens your frequencies. Think about how good you feel when you are grateful for something. It is uplifting and positive. Be grateful and always give thanks for the assistance you receive, whether you are consciously aware of the help or not.

CONNECTION

Connection is the part of the practice that plugs you in and turns you on to higher consciousness. If you have meditated or prayed, you have already practiced plugging in by drawing into the higher consciousness through the top of your head and then grounding it into the earth. The difference with Mindkeeping is that you are also turning on the life force. Doing this creates a connection or circuit between your mind, body, and spirit or you, the physical world, and the non-physical world. The connection prepares you for lumen consciousness. The diagrams below show you how to plug in, turn on, and input this intelligence.

PLUGGING IN

Imagine a large triangle of light sitting above your head. Draw it down through the top of your head, through your body, and into the earth. This light is the source of life that sustains you in the body. This light carries wisdom, understanding, and knowledge. By consciously drawing this light into you, you move it out of the ether, or nonphysical plane, and into the physical for you to use. Pulling it into the earth grounds the energy like a lightning rod and plugs you into the energy source.

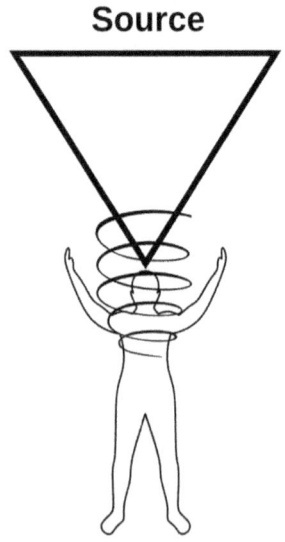

Source

TURNING ON

Turning on draws in the life force, giving you power. It allows you to take the intelligence of the source and turn it into something tangible, like taking an idea and making it a physical reality. Remember that the source and the force are part of you and are always connected. It is part of your built-in mind system; however, practicing the setup strengthens this connection on a conscious level, giving you the confidence to use this energy in your daily life.

Imagine a large triangle of energy emerging from the earth. This triangle nurtures you just as the earth nurtures a tree, giving you everything you need to grow and flourish. See it flow up from the ground, into you, and rooting itself back into the source.

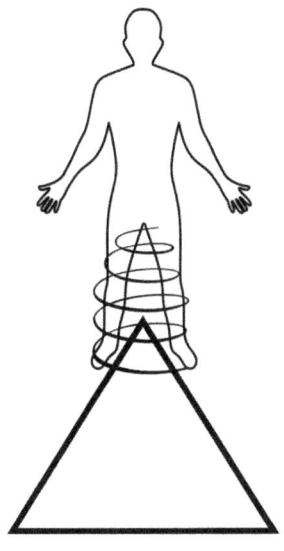

Force

SET THE COURSE (INPUT)

After you draw in the source and force, it is time to set your Course to lumen. Think of it as your mind on Wi-Fi with access to more information than you previously experienced. To set the Course, you have to input your intention.

103

What is your intention? What do you want your mind to do? Do you want to heal, gain more knowledge, have better relationships, or make more money? Whatever it is you desire, you have to ask for it. You have to make it happen, and when you do, life will change in subtle and extraordinary ways. You will experience yourself from a higher perspective as you realize you are more in control of your life than you thought because you choose what happens next.

When my students don't know what to ask for, I suggest they use this intention as a go-to: "I now merge with the source and force as I set my Course to awaken, evolve, and heal." You can't go wrong with that. That covers all the bases that you need to move forward. It works in all situations and circumstances. For instance, if you want to increase your income in this practice, you say, think, or feel you want more income. As you set your intention, you set the energy (E-motion) for change. Now, please remember that this will not happen simultaneously. Still, once practiced, you will start to see and understand what is holding you back from making more money. You will evolve into a better circumstance that will heal the problem that you had in the first place. It is all pretty easy once you get the hang of it.

Remember, the setup is the most essential step in your practice. If you only did this and nothing else, you would still have great results; however, when you add the technology, it changes your life because it is how you adjust your frequencies. Once you are comfortable setting up, the whole process will take about a minute or two. Anyone can fit that into their schedules, even if you do it while brushing your teeth.

For those already proficient in meditation, keep doing what works for you, and add any part of the setup you may not be currently doing.

SOURCE + FORCE = COURSE

Source + force = Course. I created this equation to help you with the setup.

It's easy to remember and reminds you of what you are doing and why you are doing it.

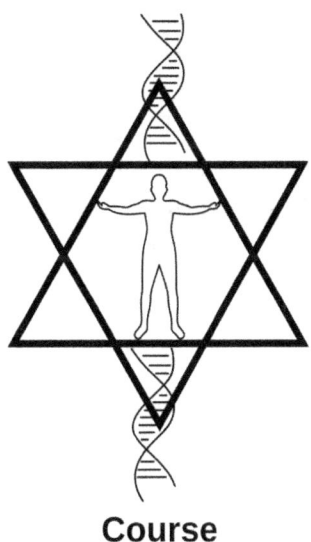

Course

For those that want an alternate or shortened version of the setup, substitute *source, force* and *Course* with *me, myself,* and *I*.

For instance:

      I plug the light into ME

      I turn on my SELF

      I now input my intention for the purpose of _____

The connected system will look like a six-sided star once you have drawn the source down via one triangle and the force up to you via another. This six-sided star is your "phone case" or lumen body. Your lumen body overlays your physical body, protecting you as you travel through the networks of higher consciousness. This connection is where the physical and nonphysical harmonize to strengthen and fortify the system. As stated previously, if you do nothing else but set up each day, you are already ahead of the game because you are connecting consciously to your lumen mind.

COMPLETED SETUP

The diagram below is an example of before, during, and after the setup. You can see the changes from the human mind to the lumen mind. The lumen mind has a more extensive network, giving you access to more information and knowledge.

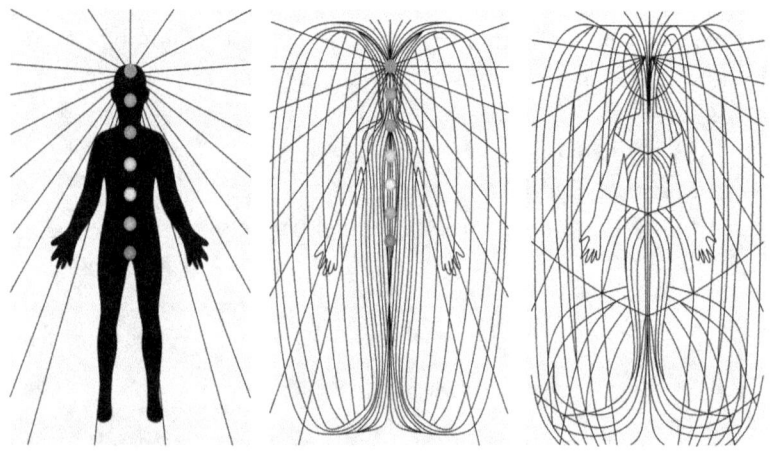

ORGANIZE

One of the most significant problems people have is a racing mind. They can't seem to shut down their thoughts. Their minds are always thinking or worrying about something. They have trouble focusing, remembering, and sleeping. When they don't get enough rest, they become irritable, and their stress levels climb. Organizing your mind helps minimize that by asking specific questions to get you to focus on one thing at a time instead of ten things at once. It also helps to tune out the noise long enough to move through the process.

Organizing your mind starts with SELF-REFLECTION. When you can see the problem, you can change it. People tend to get angry without knowing what they are angry about. That's a problem. It's not unusual to think you know the reason only to find out later that it was completely different. Remember, your mind tricks you, but your feelings don't. Sometimes, what you think to be true is just an illusion, but how you feel about something is accurate because it is internal and yours, not external and someone else's.

Remember, you are the Mindkeeper. You are responsible and accountable for everything you think, feel, believe, act, and react to. No matter how much you want to point the finger at others, it will always come back to you. It is your thoughts, your feelings, your beliefs, your actions, and your reactions that you are organizing. Keep that in mind, and the rest is easy.

As you self-reflect, you will ask yourself these questions:

- What is bothering me?
- Am I blaming others or taking responsibility?
- Is this a habit?
- Does it make me feel good or bad?

Remember that I am breaking all these segments into little sound bites, making it seem more complicated. Still, I want you to know the nitty-gritty so you have all the information you need to make your practice successful. In the following chapters, I will show you how to streamline the process, making it realistic and fun.

What is bothering you?

Although there can be several answers to this question, take one subject or problem at a time. Think about your life. What is bothering you? Is it your spouse, children, work, finances, feeling unappreciated or overlooked? It can be anything, and it doesn't have to be significant. It can be the small things that add up. Whatever is the biggest thorn in your side, make that the issue you reflect upon.

Am I blaming others or taking responsibility?

Taking responsibility for your actions can be challenging. It's not that you don't want to be responsible; most do. But sometimes, you don't realize that you do not own up to what is yours. Do you remember the old saying "the devil made me do it"? That's just one example of how you take yourself out of the mix. How about "It's his fault that I am this way," or "If she wasn't such a bitch, I wouldn't be this way," or even "I am a product of my childhood or my environment." Although those statements may have some truth, they all blame others. What is your responsibility in all of this? What makes you an active participant in your life, and what does the devil have to do with your actions? Your actions are still yours; you are ultimately responsible no matter how you look at them.

One word that makes me cringe every time I hear it is *narcissist.* When people tell me that their spouse, child, or whomever is a narcissist, my first question is, are they narcissistic, or are you calling them selfish because they are not agreeing with you? Even if they are narcissistic, what is your role in the relationship? Do you sit there and let that person walk all over you, or do you stand up for yourself and not allow it to happen? I know that sounds contrite and cut and dried, and most relationships are more complex than that. I am deliberately exaggerating the point that your role plays in the relationship. An active participant will drive away from the dysfunction with the understanding that it may not be easy, but it is necessary. The inactive participant is the passenger in the relationship and will put up with whatever the other person throws at them. That's not to say that role won't change eventually, but when you don't know how to move on from the situation in a way that makes you feel safe, you will likely stay put.

What about being a product of your childhood or upbringing? Show me someone who says they had the perfect childhood, and I'll show you a pig flying. Okay. A few of you are out there, but it is not the majority. Unfortunately, many never grow beyond that childhood and perpetuate the same negative patterns. Some will want better for themselves and seek out what they can do to achieve it.

Is this a habit?

Believe it or not, there are habits that you create or develop that you are not even aware of. You develop them because you may have learned something when you were young without questioning it, which later becomes a habit. Here's an example. There is a story of the woman who made a large roast for the holidays. The first year, she bought the roast, cut off the end, and put it in the oven. She did the same thing in the second and third years, too. In the fourth year, she did the same thing, only this time, her aunt was visiting from out of town.

When her aunt saw what she was doing, she asked, "Why did you cut off the end of the roast?" The woman replied, "Because that is how Grandma made it. Cutting off the end makes it taste better." The aunt laughed and said, "Yes, that is how Grandma made it but not because it made the roast better. She cut it because her pan was too small to fit the roast!" You see, this woman made it a habit to cut the roast because she thought it was the way it was supposed to be. She never considered it was for any other reason. Now, the roast stays intact, and the habit of cutting it to improve it no longer exists. You see, sometimes you do things just because you think that is the way to do something.

Sometimes, people are in the habit of being angry or sad. It isn't so much that they feel that way, but they have been a certain way for so long that they don't think to change it or know how to change it. Consider what is bothering you and ask yourself, is this a habit? Am I in the habit of being angry, frustrated, or stressed? You will be surprised to find how many habits you keep that aren't yours, such as the woman with the roast. Sometimes, your habits are hand-me-downs. You have acquired them from family, friends, or society. Check yourself and leave those nasty habits at the door. You don't need them anymore.

Does it make me feel good or bad?

The most critical question is, how does this make you feel? Does it make you feel good or bad? Use this question for everything, and watch how you grow. If you know how you feel, you can change it, and breaking it down into good or bad takes out the gray areas, such as *I feel good, but….*

How does whatever is on your mind make you feel? It doesn't matter what your question is; the answer matters.

How does your job make you feel? How does your spouse or marriage make you feel? How do your finances make you feel?

How do your kids make you feel? How do you feel about your body? Asking the questions helps you to discern the truth about your situation or circumstance. Your mind will play tricks on you, but your feelings don't lie.

Do you remember the optical illusion analogy? You may swear you saw something that isn't there because your mind sees it through a distorted lens. How about your hearing? Did you hear what you wanted, or did you hear a sound bite of information and draw a conclusion based on part of the story instead of the story? Your mind sees and hears what it wants to. It is adaptable to the situation and environment. Your feelings are different; they are not always truthful, but you will know if something doesn't feel right.

You know if something makes you feel good or bad. You may not substantiate the circumstances, but know how you feel about it. For instance, you may feel jealous toward your partner. Your partner may not be doing anything wrong; however, you still feel jealous. The feeling makes you feel bad. Bad is how you feel about the situation, whether based on truth or not. However, you still feel something is off, which tells you something is off within you. No two minds are alike when it comes to feelings. They may be similar, but what you feel belongs to you only. It is your body that is feeling it. Knowing how you feel will always lead you to your truth, even if it isn't truthful in the moment.

Your feelings are how your mind communicates with you. It tells you what is in and out of sync with your system. A happy, healthy system feels good about most situations; an unhealthy system feels bad and continues to create misfortune because it either isn't aware of it or doesn't know how to correct it.

ANALYZE

Analyze through self-empathy. You know empathy is the ability to understand and share the feelings of others. Self-empathy is the ability to understand and share your feelings. In analyzing, you come to know the frequencies you carry.

The three principles of Mindkeeping are to live your philosophy, practice empathy, and adjust your frequencies. Now, you will learn how to practice empathy, which will help you to recognize your frequencies. Considering that everything in the universe is energy and all energy has vibrations and frequencies, this segment enables you to understand yourself from an energetic perspective and not just a physical one.

As you analyze, you will ask yourself these questions:

What/how do I feel?

Are these my feelings, or did I pick them up from someone else?

Is this what I believe, or is this learned?

Do I know why I feel this way?

Is there a trigger that I am aware of?

What and how do you feel?

You already did the "what" when you organized, but it doesn't hurt to ask yourself that question again. More importantly, how do you feel about it? How does your situation or circumstance make you feel? When I often ask that question, the response is, "I feel angry." I understand that you feel angry, but what do you feel angry about? What is it about the situation or circumstance that makes you angry? If you say you are angry and leave it at that, you never get to the problem because you have masked the problem behind anger. You are angry for a reason. What is the reason? How does it make you feel beyond the anger? Be specific. The more precise you are about your feelings, the more progress you make.

For instance, say you feel angry because you don't believe that anyone listens to you. Your reason for being angry is not anger itself but not being heard.

Not being heard is a more straightforward issue to tackle than being angry. Anger, frustration, stress, and disappointment are catchalls for the real problem. Be specific about what is bothering you and how you feel about it. The more specific you are, the faster you change because you get to the root of the problem.

Are these my feelings, or did I pick them up from someone else?

That may sound like a crazy question, but you would be amazed by how much energy you pick up from others, especially if you are empathic or highly sensitive. Empaths constantly pick up energy from those around them, usually without knowing it. If you have walked into a room of people or a place such as a big-box store and instantly felt tired, cranky, or irritable, you are likely picking up someone else's energy.

Most of my life was confusing as an empath because I thought one way and felt another. I could not figure out why until I understood I was picking up what others were feeling. My feelings were being pushed aside without me even knowing it. I could go to work in a perfect mood, but after half an hour in the office, I was miserable and angry. I didn't know what I was angry about; I only knew I was angry. It took me well into my forties to figure out why. It also made me realize that I am better off working away from people than constantly with them. Working for myself or in sales away from the office environment was a better fit. That's not to say that empathic people can't work together; however, having your own space is very beneficial for you until you know yourself well enough to create the boundaries you need not to let that happen.

You tend to put your feelings aside to make others happy, so it only makes sense that you are more in touch with how others feel than how you feel. You believe you need to compromise, and although I agree with that to a certain degree, it is not always the right thing to do. It takes age and wisdom to understand that just because someone feels a certain way, you don't have to feel that way for fear of some repercussion.

Is this what I believe, or is this learned?

Again, go back to how you feel about something. Is this how you feel, or is this what you learned? It seems like such a fundamental question, but if you stop to think about it for a moment, you will be surprised by how much influence the world has on you.

Do you feel prejudiced or biased toward something or someone? Are those your feelings, or were they handed down to you by someone else? Years ago, it was not uncommon to hear someone referred to by their race or religion. I experienced it myself in the early eighties. I was working in Passaic, New Jersey, when a little boy about seven years old walked up to me and said, "Get out of here, honky." I couldn't believe that these words came out of this little body. I wasn't offended. I knew he didn't know what he was saying as much as repeating what he had heard. I find it hard to believe that the boy naturally felt this way rather than learned it from his surroundings or environment.

Consumerism, social media, influencers, society, and your family all play a part in influencing how you feel. If you are mindful, you can avoid getting caught up in what the world says is right for you instead of what you feel is right for you. Are you quick to go along, or do you march to your own drummer? Take the time to determine your feelings about what you see and hear. Don't just agree because you want to fit in. Be an individual and let the world fit into you.

Do you know why you feel this way?

Sometimes, you know why you feel the way you do but don't know what to do. That's a start. Take that feeling and run through the SOAR process. By the time you complete it, you will begin to feel better and have a different perspective about why you felt that way in the first place.

Is there a trigger that you are aware of?

Is there something or someone that sets you off? Pay attention. Try to see if you can recognize what exactly triggers you and your reaction to those triggers. These are all clues to help you find your frequencies.

AWARENESS VS. RECOGNITION

What is the difference between awareness and recognition? For example, you can be aware of something or someone but not identify with it. Let's say you are standing in your front yard and see a woman walking down the street. You are aware it's a woman; you may even be aware of her age, hair color, and clothes, but it is not until she gets closer that you recognize it is your friend. Awareness makes you mindful, and recognition makes it personal because you can identify it.

Organizing and analyzing your mind is to recognize and identify your feelings so you can change them. Awareness doesn't do that for you; recognition does. When you realize this, you take ownership of the emotion and identify if those frequencies are helping you or hurting you.

REPAIR

The last step in the process is the repair. The repair allows you to take a feeling or frequency that is not good for you and turn it into something good through alchemy. Alchemy is the transformation of matter by taking a base metal and turning it into gold. In this case, you are not using metal; you are using the frequencies of your feelings. In other words, you are taking a thought, feeling, belief, or memory with little or no value and transmuting it into one with great value. For instance, if you are feeling rejected, that is a feeling that gives off a low frequency and makes you feel bad. By repairing that issue through alchemy, you change it from something that makes you feel bad into a higher vibration that makes you feel good, such as love.

As you repair your mind, you understand the importance of recognizing your feelings. You know the old saying: "You've got to be specific to be terrific." It helps. The more precise you are about what you feel and what you want to change, the more effective your repair will be. I also emphasize that repairing your mind is not just fixing your feelings or thoughts. Your mind is your whole system, including your thoughts, feelings, memories, fears, habits, beliefs, DNA, ancestral traits, and body.

The repair is so easy that most people can't believe it works until they try it a few times. Once they get the hang of it, it changes how they feel. The change doesn't always come in how you think it will; it is subtle and will sneak up on you. It's like you realize that you feel different, but you're unsure how or when it happened.

Remember, you are taking something that makes you feel bad, like unworthiness, and turning it into something that makes you feel good, such as confidence. Initially, you might have to fake it until you make it. You may not always feel or believe the new frequency when moving into it, but I assure you it will kick in after some practice.

Once you know what you want to change, you state the sentence below. (I have inserted the feelings *rejected* and *accepted* as an example.)

"I now release all energy attached to feeling rejected in any way, shape, or form, anywhere and everywhere in time and space from creation through infinity, and I transmute it into feeling accepted."

That's it. That is all you have to do to change your mind. By being mindful and practicing that statement, you can change anything in your life because you are changing the frequency from the source of which it began. When you practice Mindkeeping, good things start to happen for you. I have seen it repeatedly with my clients and students, not to mention myself. They change, and their lives become better and more manageable. The struggle subsides, and the good seeps in. It doesn't happen overnight, but it does occur in a relatively short amount of time.

SOAR RECAP

At the beginning of this chapter, I broke down each segment for you to better understand what you are doing and why you are doing it. It may have seemed challenging or to have too many steps, but when you put it all together again, you will see how simple and easy it is to SOAR once you know the sequence and are familiar with the questions. The whole process will take you less than two minutes to do. Of course, the longer you practice, the more proficient you become and the more changes you experience. However, you will still achieve the benefits if you only do two minutes or just the setup.

Setup: "I call upon God, Jesus, my angels, and guides to help me now. Amen" (incantation complete). ****Please feel free to use your own words.*

Source + force = Course: (plug in, turn on, input)

"I now plug into the source. I turn on the life force, and I merge the source and force as I set my Course to lumen mind within my physical body with the intention of _____ (default-awakening, evolving, and healing)."

Alternate:

"I now plug into ME, I turn on my SELF, and I set my course to lumen mind within my body with the intention of_____."

**This is essential. Be sure to do this part of the practice every day.

Organize: through self-reflection

- What is bothering me?
- Am I blaming others or taking responsibility?
- Is this a habit?
- Does it make me feel good or bad?

Analyze: through self-empathy

- How/what do I feel?
- Are these my feelings, or did I pick them up from someone else?
- Is this what I believe, or is this learned?
- Do I know why I feel this way?
- Is there a trigger that I am aware of?

Repair: through alchemy (frequency/mind/changer)

"I now release all energy attached to _____ in any way, shape, or form, anywhere and everywhere in time and space from creation through infinity, and I transmute it into _____." Use the underlined areas for the feelings you want to change from and to. For instance, you want to switch energy attached to sadness and transmute it into happiness. The first blank is what you want to change, and the second is what you want to change it to. Sometimes, you might need clarification on your feelings, so I have included a list of common emotions and feelings to help guide you if you get stuck.

Once you do this a few times and get it down pat, it should take a few minutes daily. Ideally, you will do this at the beginning of your day and before bed. Try it for a week and notice how different you feel.

FEELINGS AND EMOTIONS GUIDE

Anger	Not feeling able	Judged
Sadness	Not feeling safe	Insecure
Heartache	Overlooked	Shock
Frustration	Overwhelmed	Nervousness
Aggravation	Jealous	Trauma
Betrayal	Distrustful	Defensive
Insecurity	Vulnerable	Feeling you have to explain yourself
Financial worry	Weak	Being doubted
Not feeling loved	Alienated	Feeling doubtful
Not feeling wanted	Disappointed	Disconnected
Not feeling like you belong	Worry	Separate
Inadequate	Indifferent	Estranged
Resentful	Numb	Not good enough
Unequitable	Sad	Feeling attacked
Slighted	Hurt	Disapproval
Feeling not seen	Grief	Burdened
Feeling jilted	Sorrow	Not acknowledged
Feeling exposed	Angst	Disrespected
Overly Sensitive	Made fun of	Not taken seriously
Picked on	Rejected	

Loved	Trusting	Jubilant
Cared for	Peaceful	Successful
Cared about	Joyful	Wealthy
Wanted	Happy	Healthy

Here is the **SOAR GUIDE** to help you streamline the process.

SET UP: Breath • Invocation • Source • Force • Course (plug in/turn on/input)

ORGANIZE: Through Self-Reflection

- What's bothering me?
- Am I blaming someone, or am I taking responsibility?
- Is this a habit or something I've learned I am holding on to?
- Does this make me feel good or bad?

ANALYZE: Through Self-Empathy

- What do I feel? How do I feel?
- Are these my feelings, or did I pick them up from someone else?
- Is this what I believe, or is it learned?
- Why do I feel this way? Do I know?
- Is there a trigger?

REPAIR: Through Alchemy

I now release all energy attached to (whatever lower frequency I am feeling) *in any way, shape, or form, anywhere and everywhere in time and space from creation through infinity, and I transmute it into* (desired higher frequency).

MAKE THE PRACTICE YOUR OWN

When I created Mindkeeping, I did it as a guideline for you to follow to help you evolve. It is a reference and guide for you, not a rule. Feel free to change the wording or intention to what suits you. I have students who don't like my invocation and change it to suit their needs. By all means, make it right for you. Call in the energy that is meaningful to you. Use the icons of your religion if that is what makes you comfortable. If you are not religious, use something that has meaning, such as the earth, fairies, celestial beings, or what have you. Assemble your team and connect with them daily through your setup. There is no right or wrong way to do this if you work with benevolent energy forces.

The same goes for setting your intention. I always use this as a default, "for awakening, evolving and healing." That covers most of the bases; however, be more specific. If you intend to have more compassion, wisdom, insight, understanding, better relationships, or what have you, go for it. If you want to narrow it down even more to a feeling or circumstance gnawing at you, do that, too. The practice is yours. Do what feels right for you. At first, it will feel awkward, but once you get the hang of it, feel free to experiment a little.

TWO MINUTES A DAY

I have previously broken the process down for you and put it under the microscope for better understanding, but when all is said and done, the whole process will take you about the same amount of time it takes to brush your teeth.

About two minutes is what you need to SOAR. Once you get into the practice, you can give it more time. Giving it more time allows you to go deeper into yourself and gain greater clarity and understanding on higher levels of consciousness. However, if you only give it two minutes, you will still experience positive results. Below is an example of Mindkeeping in two minutes.

DAILY MINDKEEPING

"Create your life. Don't let life happen to you."

One of the most significant issues people tell me is consistency with their practice. Like anything else, it has to be fun or purposeful for you to want to do it. Make it fun. Look at it as the adventure of your life or the ultimate treasure hunt. Make it a reward you look forward to because it makes you feel good. Once you get past the awkwardness of learning something new, you will love how it makes you think and feel. Below are a few tips to help you with your practice.

Don't try to meditate; SOAR and everything else will come in time.

Spend two minutes daily connecting your mind, body, and spirit by doing your setup. Connecting keeps you plugged in and protected throughout your day.

Once you are consciously connected (setup), you can pull info into and away from you as needed. Think of it as your personal search engine giving you access to your higher senses and greater intelligence, wisdom, and understanding.

**Don't underestimate the power of consciously connecting through your setup. Each time you do it, you become stronger on ALL LEVELS.

After you set up, follow through with any or all of these actions daily.

- Spend two minutes a day asking yourself what you want.
- Spend two minutes organizing your thoughts and feelings. (*Is this mine? Is this how I feel? Is this a belief system?*)
- Spend two minutes asking how this situation, person, and experience make you feel. (*Is it good enough?*)
- Spend two minutes practicing the repair on any person, experience, or situation that you want to change the frequency of.
- Take deep, cleansing breaths throughout the day.
- Try journaling or writing down your thoughts, feelings, or dreams.
- Try to determine where you feel the energy (for more advanced Mindkeepers). *Do I feel it in my body, subtle bodies, chakras, grids, mental, emotional? Does it feel good or bad?*
- Determine what you want to do with that energy.
- Share your info carefully. Hang out with people who can support and uplift you. Choose how you share wisely.

Start with two minutes, then add each element until you can do the whole series. The entire series is only ten minutes long. Time is precious. If you need more time, use your toilet time; that's a perfect way to multi-task.

Two minutes a day will change your life-ten minutes a day will change your life forever.

BEFORE BED

Set up your mind and state your intentions. Try to organize, analyze, and repair. If not, don't worry about it, and don't worry if you fall asleep. Your intention is complete, and the energy will follow along accordingly. Please note you may have disrupted sleep or strange dreams due to the frequencies changing within your system. I will go into more detail about this in the next chapter.

QUICK FIXES TO RAISE YOUR ENERGY FAST AND EASY

How about this old joke: "How do you get to Carnegie Hall? Practice, practice, practice." The more you practice, the more Mindkeeping becomes a part of your daily routine. When you are a proficient Mindkeeper, you can ward off, balance, and transmute any energy that interferes with your peace and well-being. That's not to say you won't get irritated; you will. However, you can shrug off that irritation quickly and easily.

If you are in a pinch and don't have time to practice, here are a few things you can do that will instantly increase your frequencies and make you feel better.

- Deep breaths: Remember, breath is life, and deep breaths help calm you as well as relax the tension in your mind and body.
- Sing: Singing raises your frequency. You can't possibly sing and stay in a bad mood. Try it; you will see that your mood instantly changes.
- Dance: Dancing is another way of releasing tension and pressure. Express yourself. Dance like nobody is watching.
- Exercise: You all know the benefits of exercising. Take a walk, go to the gym, ride a bike. Whatever it is, you want to get your body moving.
- Get out in nature: Nothing is so soothing like a walk on the beach or a stroll through the mountains. It is invigorating and propels your energy.
- Hug a tree: This goes with getting out in nature; however, stopping to hug a tree has enormous benefits. It calms you, raises your energy, and connects you to the life force.

** Find your community: Transformation can be a vulnerable time. Make sure you keep company with those who support and elevate you.

** Stay in the present. It's okay to imagine or reference experiences you've had, but don't stay there. Grab your info and go.

CHAPTER 10

Managing Expectations

EVERY FLOWER STARTS FROM A SEED

Your spiritual journey will be fun and exciting. There will be a lot of information before you and a lot of junk you have to sift through. I can tell you from my experience it took me years to learn how to discern truth from fiction, and it also took me years to learn how to trust myself and my instincts. Discernment will be one of your most challenging tasks, but once learned, it will be your greatest ally.

In my younger years, I was fascinated by how some people seemed to know things of a spiritual or mystical nature while others didn't. How did they know? Were they picking up on our subtle clues, or did they have a more profound and direct connection to God? It is a question I have sought the answer to for years, and as many people I have asked that question to, I have received as many different answers. It is all a matter of opinion based on the person's experience. Some I asked were gifted and gave me great insight, while others were testing their gifts, and I was their guinea pig. You will have much of this, especially when you begin, but I urge you: try everything. Try as much as you can. Try as many modalities as possible and talk to as many people you can. Join uplifting groups, and beware of those who think they know it all. How will you learn? Ask yourself how you feel about it. Does it feel right for you, or is there something off?

In my earlier years, I would try almost anything. I would seek out readers, healers, shamans, and herbalists. I would listen to what each person had to say and want to believe them, but more times than not, what they predicted did not come true. We all want to hear about the good stuff. Who wouldn't want to hear that love or money is coming your way, but is that information practical? How is this helping you? What information are you receiving that enables you to be a better person? What information are you receiving that helps you solve a problem, and what information allows you to improve your life?

These are some of the factors to consider when trying new things. As a healer, I want you to know why you do the things you do. Once you understand that, you no longer have the need or desire to hold on to it. Most times, people aren't aware of how or why they self-sabotage. Knowledge is power, so when you seek counsel from anyone, make sure it is powerful. Trust how you feel about the information. Does it feel authentic, or is it just wishful thinking?

Determine how you feel about each experience you have. When you try a new herb, ask yourself if it's doing the trick for you. Does it make you feel better? Does it do what it claims to do? When you try essential oils, ask yourself the same. *Does this make me feel better? Is it helping me in some way? Is it practical?* Do the same with flower essences, crystals, energy healing, meditation, yoga, life coaching, and anything you try. *How does this make me feel?* Do you feel different in a positive way? If it feels good, keep going. If it feels wrong, there may be a better fit for you. There is no right or wrong. Each individual is attracted to different things for different reasons.

I never cared for herbs. I have tried them many times but have yet to feel the effects, but I like flower essences and essential oils. I don't feel any significant difference using essential oils, but I like the smell, and they are natural, unlike perfumes.

There are so many healing techniques as well. Try them all, but ask yourself what you get in return. There are many practitioners, and not all are equally qualified. You can go to a Reiki master who just had a weekend course and earned a certificate, or you can go to one who has been practicing for many years. They each bring something unique to the table. It is up to you to determine which best suits your needs.

Only you can determine how that person and technique makes you feel. There are a lot of qualified people out there, and there are a lot who aren't. Time doesn't necessarily make a person good. What makes a healer good is their ability to dive in and heal their issues. The more depth the healer has, the deeper the healing you will receive. A seed has to go through a lot of dirt before it becomes a flower. Is your healer a seed or flower? Even the mighty oak started as a seed. Trust yourself. Trust how you feel about it and move on. Don't put your faith solely on another person. It is your life and your decision to make. You have to determine how you want to live your life.

Think of it as being at a buffet table. There are things you will try that you like and things you try that you don't like, and then there are things that you are on the fence about. That's okay. It's all part of the process.

HOW DO YOU KNOW IF YOU ARE AWAKENING?

One thing I always say about energy and healing is it is subtly profound. It won't smack you in the face; don't expect to hear a booming voice from the clouds. It doesn't work that way. It is gentle. It comes up on you like a gentle breeze that you hardly notice, yet it changes you so much that you can't help but notice.

It creeps in when you least expect it and has a lasting effect that makes you scratch your head in wonder. You may not consciously feel different. You may not have noticed anything at all, then out of nowhere, you do something positive that you may not have had the courage to do before, such as speak up for yourself or make a significant change.

It can be as simple as just saying no. Maybe you have felt used at work or had too much responsibility because you didn't want to say no. Perhaps you were fearful that you would not be seen as a hard worker or dedicated employee if you didn't go the extra mile and do the extra work, even if it meant compromising yourself and your family. Then, one day, you are asked to do something you don't want to do or is too much for you, and out of the blue, you say no. *I'm sorry. That is too much for me with what I already have going on.* You will say it, and you will be shocked that you said it, and at the same time, you will feel empowered because you spoke up for what was best for you.

My clients say to me all the time, "You aren't going to believe this, but I spoke up and said how I felt, and not only that, I was shocked by how they received it. They not only heard me, but they understood where I was coming from and why. I don't know what got into me, but I did it and feel great."

"Well," I tell them. "You got into you."

That's what happens when you are awakening. Life and everything in it become more equitable.

I am not telling you to say no just for the hell of it; this is just an example of awakening at play. Another example is when you begin to notice more synchronicity in your life. You receive a call from someone you were thinking about. You run into an old friend you haven't seen in a while, and they have a connection to someone who can help you somehow.

You will start to see numbers in sequences. 222,333,444, and, of course, 11:11. You will wake up in the middle of the night, and it will be the same time. You will repeatedly see other signs, such as cardinals or certain animals.

Issues that you had, such as anxiety, depression, worry, fear, and financial pressures, start to diminish. You notice you feel happier and not as anxious. You can be more in the present and not worry so much about the past or future.

Awakening lifts your self-esteem and value, which raises your finances. You notice the squeeze isn't so tight. You recognize good things are starting to happen for you, as well as new opportunities. You will see life is brighter. The sky will seem bluer, and the trees will seem greener. The flowers will appear more colorful, too. Little by little, these are subtle signs of awakening, but the most powerful of all is you noticing you.

You will start to notice things or people that bother you that didn't bother you in the past. You will see the subtle nuances of things and pick up details about the person or situation you couldn't distinguish. You will experience not fitting into places and situations you used to, as if you outgrew a piece of clothing and want to replace it with another.

You remember things you once enjoyed and either revisit them or try new things. You feel more happy than sad and more hopeful than depressed. You start to see the forest through the trees and can make decisions based on a higher perspective and more dimensional information. You have more epiphanies and aha moments that help you understand yourself and the world around you. Awakening is a process of going within and finding the awakened you. The further you go, the more precise you become until one day, your energy is no longer subtle but unmistakable, obvious, and intentionally profound.

INCREDIBLE THINGS HAPPEN WHEN YOU AWAKEN YOUR MIND

There are a lot of cool things that happen as you awaken your mind. Most start with the sentence "You're not going to believe this," or "You're going to think I'm crazy." I don't think anybody is crazy. If I did, I would have had to institutionalize myself years ago. When you have a unique or different experience, enjoy it unless it is dark, which I will cover later in this book.

When you go beyond, expect to be surprised sometimes. My earliest memory of something strange was when I was about a year and a half or two years old. I had just come out of the crib and into a double bed with my sister. I don't know if I fell out or what happened, but I landed on my head. I don't remember the incident, but my mother held me with my father looking over her. They both had this look of "oh shit" in their eyes, and I remember thinking in my voice that I have now, *What the hell are you looking at?* I could not figure out their problem, and even though I was an infant, my mind was as mature as today. I didn't find out until afterward that the concern on their faces was because I had turned blue, and they didn't know if I would be okay. To me, I was fine. It was they who had the problem.

This same sort of thing happened several times. I'm not referring to the falling part but the conscious voice that took over my childish mind when the opportunity presented itself. I have had a lifetime of strange but true incidents. Below are a few that come to mind.

When I lived in Arizona, there was a mountain behind my house. I climbed that mountain every day and meditated before I went to work. One day, as I was meditating, a swarm of bees appeared. I didn't know what to do, and running would be a stupid option, so I opened my hands, palms up, and two bees landed. Each in a palm. They stood there, completely still, as if to tell me something. They stayed for about five minutes and left. I wasn't afraid they would sting me; I thought the whole thing was mystical and strange. I focused my energy on bees for a while to ensure I got the info they sent me.

Another time, out of nowhere, I started seeing colors around people. It began one day when I dropped my kids off at daycare. The daycare owner was standing outside, greeting the children as they walked in, and all I could see around her was green. She was completed green. I could see her face, but that was it. I couldn't tell you what she was wearing or anything else because it was all green. After dropping off the kids, I headed to my first appointment for work. When I arrived at the customer's door, she appeared purple. She must have thought I was nuts because I couldn't look at her. I was distracted. Every time she moved, it was as if someone was applying a fresh coat of paint to her body. This experience went on for days. It was bizarre. Then, as quickly as it came, it ended, just like that. I never had that experience again. I don't know why it happened, as I don't work with auras or colors, but it was an exciting and disturbing experience nonetheless.

There are so many experiences, I could write another book on that topic alone, but what I found to be genuinely fascinating is how many people have encountered Jesus, Buddha, the saints, and otherworldly beings. When I had my encounter, I thought it was unique, only to find it happens frequently to others. It shows how truly connected we are, and if you sincerely ask for divine guidance and intercession, trust that it will happen.

NOT-SO-GREAT THINGS HAPPEN WHEN YOU AWAKEN YOUR MIND

For every action, there is a reaction. It is the same thing with awakening your mind. The more you awaken, the more you have to deal with the issues that caused your mind to be closed in the first place. Sometimes, this plays out in ways that could be more comfortable.

When I first started Mindkeeping, I had a headache every day for a year. Discomfort doesn't happen to everyone, but it does happen. Excessive and old energies must find ways to release as the body's cells, thoughts, and emotions expand. For me, at that time, it was headaches. I knew what it was, so I wasn't alarmed. As you go through this process, you will experience many things that could be more pleasant. The process can be easy or hard depending on the individual and their willingness to let go and let flow.

When you don't know what is happening, you may automatically think something is wrong with you, such as having unusual aches and pains, colds or diarrhea, weird dreams, restless nights, canker sores, rashes, dizziness, and tiredness. All of these are side effects of awakening. The more you increase your light and awaken, the stranger you may feel.

One of my clients' most significant side effects is feeling on shaky ground or not feeling grounded. Part of this is because they are no longer where they were and not quite where they are going. It's a transitional purgatory of old habits, relationships, and roles they played into the new, more elevated relationships and parts they will play. Think of it as the dressing room between acts of a play. You take off one costume and put on another. It can be uncomfortable if you haven't played that role before because you don't know what it feels like and how receptive others will be toward the new you.

The good news is it only lasts a short time and is not so overwhelming that it impedes your progress. As you continue to move forward, you will feel a little different in a good way. Once you integrate and assimilate the new energies, you are good to go until you decide to do it again.

I don't want to scare you or make you think that this is a real problem because it's not. Most of my clients have minor side effects, if any.

It is possible and probable in some ways and circumstances. My rule of thumb is to give it a three-day time frame. If you are working on yourself or having work done to you and start to feel a side effect, consider that the work may be the reason. If it does not subside in three days, get it checked. The discomfort often equates to the expansion and understanding that you will move through it faster and effortlessly.

Another side effect to consider when evolving is nightmares and strange dreams. Don't be fazed if this happens; it can work in your favor. For instance, if I am working on a client with deep emotional issues or PTSD, I often suggest they release the pent-up emotions through their dreams. It is much easier on their system and comforts them, knowing they don't have to replay the trauma. They rarely have nightmares, but they have interesting dreams we can discuss and interpret if needed.

DON'T COMPARE YOURSELF

Please don't compare yourself to anyone, especially regarding your spiritual growth. The only person you should listen to is yourself. I used to sit in spiritual development classes, listen to people talk about their psychic experiences, and wonder what was wrong with me when I didn't have that experience. There was nothing wrong with me. I was comparing myself to their experiences. We all have a different skill set. Some of you are more empathic than others. Some are more clairvoyant. Some are more clairaudient, and some don't get it at all. None of it is right or wrong. It is just how you interpret energy and information. It's like being in school. Some are visual learners, and others are better at reading. Everyone learns and develops at a different pace. Don't get stuck in that belief that you are "doing "it" wrong." There is no wrong. There is only experience, and how you experience energy and your relationship to that energy is your unique signature.

DON'T DECEIVE YOURSELF

When you begin your Mindkeeping journey, you want to be mindful of your deception. It is not that you are intentionally deceitful, but habits can be tricky to break, especially if you have been doing them for a long time. Recognizing the deception takes time and effort, so be kind to yourself.

For instance, Janie came to me because she felt stuck. She had a career but wanted to do something more meaningful, like be a healer or coach. Every time she tried to move forward, she would get severe headaches and body aches, which prevented her from moving forward.

She had been a spiritual seeker for some time, so she already knew about energy and its effects, and I was not the only practitioner she was seeing. She had an entire routine of seeing healers, readers, and massage therapists and practicing yoga, meditation circles, and drumming. When I would work on her, she felt great, but a day or two later, she was back to where she'd started. I couldn't figure it out initially, but I noticed a pattern. The pattern was she didn't want to take responsibility for herself. She wanted the other practitioners to do it for her. When I brought this to her attention, she thought I was crazy. She said, "What do you mean? I do all this stuff for myself. I go here and there and do this and that," but what was she doing for herself? Was she looking within? Was she self-reflecting? Was she trying to organize and analyze her thoughts and feelings to change herself, or was she letting everyone else find the answers for her? She could see the pattern she created by breaking it into little bites. She understood that she had to participate in her growth to be more. She began to realize that her decisions to be what she wanted were hers to make, not ours to make for her. She accepted that if she didn't participate actively in her own life, it would keep her in the same place, stuck. That is not to say that you shouldn't seek help. By all means, do so, but don't let it be a dictatorship. Allow it to be a collaboration between you and your practitioner. Your practitioner should be able to help you connect the dots if they are well-practiced enough; there is no doubt it will help you become stronger.

Janie became stronger as she actively participated in her life and made better decisions for her future. She didn't like it initially because looking at emotions was hard. After recognizing the problem, Janie stopped deceiving herself and began to empower herself. In time, her headaches stopped, and she could move forward in her desired direction.

Janie felt good because she understood her decisions were hers and not someone else's. If she didn't like a decision, all she had to do to correct it was make a different decision. Being an active participant made her feel good about herself and gave her confidence she'd never had before.

You may ask why she didn't heal from all her work. In some ways, she did because it brought her to a point where she could face herself; however, if her lesson was to take responsibility and empower herself, I could only lead her to water. It was up to her if and when she wanted to drink. Rest assured, whether you feel ready or not, the energy given will stay with you and help you when the time is right.

CHALLENGES

What challenges can you expect to encounter? In addition to the aches, pains, and interrupted sleep I mentioned earlier, one of your biggest challenges will be with the people around you. As you change, so do they. In some cases, it is for the better; in others, it is not. It is not unusual for those close to you to rebel in some way if they feel threatened by your changes. For instance, let's say you are an enabler and have allowed your family to walk over you. You could do all the work around the house or pay all the bills. One day, you wake up and say, "I've had it. No more. From now on, everyone in this household has to carry their weight." This time, you mean it. It is not just an empty threat but a reality. You are on strike. Your family might react negatively to the new you. They may tell you that you are wrong or try to sabotage you somehow. If you know what to expect, you will stay the course. If not, you might fall back into the same pattern as before.

If someone has an investment in you being weak, they will try to keep you that way. It's not that they are being mean. They don't know how to react to you if you are not the same person. The energy dynamic has changed, which means they cannot relate to you in the same way as before.

It could be something so simple as outgrowing your friends. When you change, everything around you changes too, and what used to be good enough is no longer good enough. It isn't devastating or horrible.

It is something to be mindful of when you are evolving to give you a reference point that you are on the right track.

SELF-JUDGMENT

Do you know this is the number one reason you have problems? You judge yourself about everything. You think you are too tall, short, fat, skinny, not strong enough, not good enough, not smart enough, not rich enough, and any other derogatory thing you can think of. It's ridiculous, and it makes you crazy. You cannot possibly live up to the images and expectations you have created for yourself. Looking at yourself, you will notice that half of those expectations didn't even come from you. You acquired them from your family, friends, and society. If your family thought you should be a certain way, you tried to live up to that. If society says you should be a certain way, you try to live up to it. Your friends, not so much, but a certain amount of comparing leads to judgment.

When working with someone who says, "I should have," I stop them immediately and ask, "You should have, what?" Most often, the answer is "I should have known better." Why should you have known better? If you knew better, you wouldn't have done what you did in the first place. How could you possibly know something you have yet to learn? You are judging yourself based on the past, not on the present. In the present, you know. In the past, you didn't.

Who cares what you did in your past? Nobody is judging you, but you. Everyone has a history. Every one of us has things we regret or feel remorseful about, but we must move on. If you have learned from those experiences, there is no reason to hold on to them anymore. Accept that you have changed. You are no longer that person in the past. You may have a history, but you are not in the past. You've changed. When you were twenty, you were no longer the person you were at ten. You would not do the same things at forty that you did when you were twenty because you grew. You matured. You have more information to draw from. You can't blame a child for not knowing what an adult knows. So stop judging yourself for not having had the proper information to draw upon. You've grown, you've learned, and you are better for it, and that is a beautiful thing.

There are a lot of bad things that happened to some of you in childhood. That is not your fault, no matter what you think or feel. You may have known something was wrong but did not have the resources within you to do anything about it, so you blame and judge yourself for the rest of your life for things that, at that time, you could not control or did not have the emotional or mental means and maturity to change. We stay stuck in the agony of judgment. always thinking we should have known better and somehow believing we are to blame.

Even those of you on the flip side of the coin eventually grow up and realize that what you did was unkind. You probably didn't do what you did out of malice but out of a desire to have power so you didn't feel powerless, yet you still judge yourself for believing you should have known better. Again, if you did, you would not have been mean but compassionate to yourself and others.

Blaming yourself is another form of judgment. I have had clients blame themselves for things they had no control over yet somehow feel it was their fault for not doing enough. Self-judgment causes your burdens to become overwhelming and take you over. You play over and over in your head the scenes you think will create a different outcome, all because you thought you should do more.

How could you do more? If it were to be, it would have been. The expectations exceed the possibilities, and you can never live up to or measure up to what you have created. You judge yourself for not being good enough, and that is not true.

DON'T APOLOGIZE FOR HOW YOU FEEL!

I used to be an apologizer. I apologized for everything. I'm sorry about this. I'm sorry about that. Until one day, I realized that I was apologizing for things that weren't even mine to apologize for. I started asking myself, *what the hell am I apologizing for?* I hadn't done anything wrong, yet I still felt the need to say sorry. It was a conditioned response, one I learned early in childhood. It was a way of keeping peace. Conflict scared me, and to avoid it, I would apologize. I would even apologize to others for how they perceived me. I would apologize if it weren't in the light they thought I should be. I apologized for being a tomboy when someone said I wasn't ladylike enough. I said I was sorry for being good at sports. I apologized for not being thin enough, popular, or capable. A few times, someone approached me and said, *you think who you are.* I think who I am? What does that mean? I'm just working or minding my own business. What had I done to elicit that response? I would piss people off without knowing how or why and apologize for it. I got so used to apologizing for being me that I stopped being me and started being whatever I thought would please others.

I always felt wrong. I always thought things were my fault or took the blame for something I didn't do. If you weren't pleased, I would apologize as if I had any control over your happiness. If someone was angry, it was my fault for not helping enough or being there. No matter what the circumstance, I felt I needed to say I was sorry about it. That's not to say I didn't have my share of stuff that I did need to apologize for; however, when you constantly apologize for feeling a certain way or just being yourself, you eventually stop being yourself.

You attract people who play into those beliefs when you feel this way. You attract those that make you feel insecure. To avoid conflict, you allow them to mentally and emotionally abuse you, and what do you do? You apologize for it. It is a vicious cycle of gaslighting that took me years to understand and overcome. It's not your fault; you weren't aware when you stopped being yourself and believing that you matter.

You have become so conditioned to go along for the ride that you stopped driving yourself. You have given your specialness away to others, and then you apologize for not being enough. You know more about what others want than what you want, and then you say you're sorry for not being happy. You deserve more. You deserve to feel good about yourself because you are the only one in your universe, which is extraordinary.

It's time to change, and with change comes challenges. The biggest challenge is understanding and believing that what you feel matters. Your feelings are your direct connection to your spirit.

Each of us has our unique set of circumstances and feelings. Many people can experience similar feelings, but no two people have the same feelings. Like snowflakes, they are individual, and each individual's feelings matter more than you can imagine. It doesn't matter who you are or what you do. Your feelings are essential to your individuality and well-being.

YOUR FEELINGS ARE YOUR SUPERPOWER

When you know how you feel and accept those feelings, be they good or bad, you can change them. You can't change what you are not in touch with, and as long as you allow others to dictate how you should feel, you will feel lost. You will feel incomplete. You will feel depressed, resentful, and unhappy.

Again, it is not your fault. It is the lesson you need to realize that your feelings are important because it is the connection between your mind, body, and spirit. Your feelings are the direct line to your needs for your evolution and happiness. It's time to be the driver of your life instead of the passenger in someone else's. Once you take the wheel, you will never need to apologize for being you again.

GROW ORGANICALLY

Don't push yourself to change. Let the changes happen naturally. Everything you want will come in time, and that time is not for you to determine. It is for nature to determine. Think of a flower. You plant the seed in the dirt and don't expect it to pop up overnight; however, you are almost sure it will happen eventually. When farmers grow their crops, they don't sit around yelling, "Come on, come on already!" They set it and forget it. It would help if you did the same. If you are doing the work to evolve, you will grow. Everything is in its own time. If you push, you can hurt yourself. Be kind to yourself, your body, and your mind, and trust that all is in divine order.

REFERENCE POINTS

I love reference points and pointing them out to my clients. Whenever you have a growth spurt, use it as a reference point or guide to help you along your path. For instance, a reference point can be anything from seeing colors more vibrantly or recognizing something about yourself or someone else you hadn't noticed before. Some clients have mystical experiences that make them feel good or bring joy. When it happens, remember it, but don't try to force it to happen again. Let it happen and flow naturally, and let them remind you of what it feels like to be in your lumen mind.

Chapter 11

Being Empathic

O nce upon a time, many years ago, I was connected to everything. I was so interconnected that I could talk to the trees. I knew what others were feeling and could anticipate what they would do. I could feel the beat of the music a split second before I heard it and could wish for something and watch it appear within a few days. Maybe not in the form I had anticipated, but it was there nonetheless.

Then, one day, it all disappeared. Or at least it seemed that way. I'm unsure if it was because I couldn't take the emotional turmoil around me or because of the pain and shame I carried with me. Either way, I had lost myself and have spent the rest of my life desperately trying to find my way back.

I had secrets. My whole life was a secret. I never told my parents anything. Mainly because back then, you didn't discuss issues with your parents. I didn't speak to my siblings or friends about it because I didn't want anyone to know my secrets. I was ashamed and didn't want to get in trouble for doing something I wasn't supposed to do.

I felt desperate for a connection but turned to the wrong places or people to find it. The need to connect led me down a path of more secrets. Secrets were my kryptonite. They robbed me of my power and potential. They took everything good away from me and left me feeling empty.

One day, amid my emptiness, I found a memory that led me to a feeling. I followed this feeling down a path that led me back to the trees. Every day, I would focus on this feeling and build on it until I had a solid foundation. Brick by brick, I would make my foundation. Day after day, month after month, year after year, until the day came that I was so strong that no force could ever take me away from me.

I had finally come full circle. Free from secrets and walls that bind me and into the knowledge and mastery of healing myself that led me to the power to help others heal too. Healing is easy once you know how, and since I've done the groundwork, all you have to do is follow the path. The life of an empath is not always easy, but I guarantee it is more fulfilling than you could ever imagine.

EVERYONE IS EMPATHIC

Empathy is how we communicate on a soul level. We are all souls, and we are all empathic. Empathy is how you feel about something, and telepathy is how you know it. Empathy and compassion are in each one of us. No one is exempt. No one is special or more special than the other. No one is more spiritual; there is no such thing. You are all souls connected to spirit, so how can anyone be more than the other? It's impossible.

Don't be fooled by the spiritual "experts." The ones that think they know everything because they have a little knowledge under their belts. That's not to say they don't know anything. Of course, they do, but nobody knows better than you what you need. It is okay to seek counsel, healing, mentoring, and whatever you need, but use your self-empathy to decide what feels true.

The most complex challenge is not being a follower but a leader and keeper of your mind. Many of you have yet to learn how to make decisions for yourself. You believe giving is better than receiving, and it is best not to go against the flow, but is that always the correct answer for you? We all want to be cooperative and be team players, but when is it time to form your team? That's where your real power lies. To know what you want, make healthy boundaries, and make the right choices. In your ability to feel what you need and follow that lead, you are doing the best and most loving thing for you and those around you. Sometimes, your decisions will create resistance. That's okay. Are you strong and convicted enough to yourself to withstand that storm? If so, you will notice that you not only empower yourself, but you empower others by making them do for themselves. Empowering yourself is the ultimate win-win situation. It doesn't seem so if you are the one who opposes the changes, but I guarantee it will make you grow. Of course, everyone has free will and choice, so they also have the option not to grow. If this happens and you choose to leave a relationship or situation because it is in your best interest, that's a good thing, even if you feel bad about it. Following your heart will not always feel good. It hurts to move forward sometimes, but who changes when things are good? No one. You wait until you are at the breaking point and then do something about it.

It's hard to be empathic when you don't know what is happening inside you. It's hard to make decisions based on your wants and needs because you are also picking up the signals of everyone around you. Knowing your energy and how you feel is in your best interest so that when you pick up others' energy, you know it isn't yours to hold onto. Being sensitive to your empathy can make your life difficult until you know and understand how to interpret the information you are receiving. Think of it as being placed in a foreign land without language knowledge. Once you learn it, though, you begin to thrive.

YOU'RE NOT SCREWED UP; YOU'RE EMPATHIC

So many people come to me and say, "I don't know what's wrong with me. I am so screwed up."

I answer, "You're not screwed up, you're empathic."

You work on a different operating system from the rest of the world. It's not your fault; you didn't get the memo. How can you be screwed up if you don't know? How can you be screwed up if you speak Spanish and the rest of the world speaks English? How can you be screwed up if you don't have anyone to show you the way or understand what you need? You did the best you could. You survived.

Empathy is to feel what someone else is feeling. Putting yourself in someone else's shoes helps you better understand their feelings or perspectives. Empathy allows you to have more compassion for them or their situation.

When you are empathic or sensitive, you pick up how that person feels without consciously knowing it. It's like picking up a radio signal or tuning into a frequency, but you have no idea it affects you. It does. It changes your moods and feelings; you don't know what hit you.

Have you ever asked yourself why you did something or *Why can't I stop doing that?* It may be because you don't understand yourself. You may think you are a logical person living in a rational world, but you're not. You are an empathic person living in a logical world. Unrecognized empathy creates a problem because although everyone is empathic, only some realize it.

The world does not always make sense to those more sensitive to their empathy because the information you pick up gets crossed between your thoughts and feelings. Crossed signals create confusion or the belief that something is wrong with you. There is nothing wrong with you. You are just picking up a double set of signals. An empath communicates primarily through feelings. Linear thinking people communicate primarily through thoughts and logic, so the interpretation between the two can sometimes be confusing.

If you get stuck in that confusion, you may end up doing things you don't want to do and not know or understand why you are doing them. Your actions become impulsive and reckless. You can have a visceral reaction instead of an intentional response to life. Knowing yourself from an empathic point of view gives you control and authority over your thoughts, feelings, beliefs, actions, and reactions to life, allowing you to create the life you want instead of allowing life to happen to you.

Helping empaths is the majority of my business. Empaths flock to me because I am an empath. I understand their dilemma and know how to do the workaround. Empaths come from all walks of life and backgrounds. My client base is vast, yet they share several things, such as low self-esteem, lack of self-confidence, putting others before themselves, not speaking up for fear of not being heard or hurting someone's feelings, believing they are responsible for everyone, feeling like they have to defend themselves, and so on.

Many have an addiction or are recovering from addiction. These people feel misunderstood or believe they don't fit in. They have weird experiences that they can't explain. They are confused, feel bad about themselves, and expect they should have known better about everything they do or have done.

They feel stuck, depressed, anxious, stressed, and some have PTSD, which I believe we all have a little of. I have yet to meet someone who comes to me and isn't waiting for the other shoe to drop. It is a vicious cycle of over and over again, chasing your tale but not getting anywhere. They are never happy but not unhappy either. Just existing, hoping there is more but rudderless to get there. Confusion is the life of an empath or HSP, with moments of fleeting happiness and a lot of misinformation in between.

That's not to say they are down on their luck, incapable people. I certainly don't mean that at all. My clients are primarily professional and successful in their own right, with many outstanding skills and talents that they can finally tap into and use with confidence, trust, and insight.

Empathy can be your greatest asset. When you learn to turn it inward, you will feel comfortable in your skin and thrive in an environment that is right for you instead of trying to fit into a world that doesn't feel right. Empathic people are artists, nurturers, healers, and creatives who make the world a better place as long as they don't self-destruct because they feel broken. Being misunderstood can make you feel broken, but you are not. I assure you. Once you understand yourself and your empathic nature, you will learn to love who you are because you see the value it brings to you and the people around you.

A LIFETIME OF MIXED MESSAGES

For empathic and sensitive people, life is one big mixed message. You hear someone say something, but what you feel is entirely different. It is a lifetime of confusion and misunderstanding. Empaths want to connect. They need to feel a connection and will do whatever it takes to make it happen. That's their nature. They are feelers; they need to feel. Unfortunately for many, they can't or don't know how to discern between their feelings and those of others. They blame themselves for everything they feel, regardless of whether it is theirs or not. They will think they did something wrong or did not do it well enough. They will take things to heart and personally when, in actuality, most times, it has nothing to do with them at all.

Again. You are all empathic, but some are more in tune with that part of themselves than others. That doesn't mean they understand that part; it just means they operate from their feelings while trying to fit into a thinking world. It is an uncertain place to be and causes many to become anxious, overwhelmed, depressed, and even turn to addiction to escape. It is not that you are weak and can't cope. It is that you are hearing one message while receiving another. It's like trying to talk to a baby. They can cry and make sounds, but you must use intuition to interpret what they want and need.

You can walk into a room and feel happy or sad for no reason. You can instantly like or dislike a person without knowing why. You can quickly become overwhelmed in public places or school functions. Events such as weddings, funerals, performances, movies, or other emotionally charged things can wreak havoc on you or make you cry at the drop of a hat. You feel ashamed or embarrassed and don't understand why you feel so weak. You are not weak; you are empathic. You are picking up the emotions and feelings from everybody and everything around you.

As an empath, you can also be very defensive because you feel as if you are being judged or critiqued about everything you do. It feels like an attack to you, for which you need to defend yourself. You take everything to heart and even sometimes out of context. For instance, someone can walk up to you most innocently and say something like "Nice haircut," and you take it as if it looks terrible. You misinterpreted the message. You took it as an insult when all that person meant by that statement was "I like your hair."

NOT AN EXCUSE TO BE AN ASS

I often hear people say, "I'm an empath," or "I am highly sensitive.

That is why I am the way I am." I say yes and no to that. You must know yourself. Your life is your responsibility, and it is up to you to live the life you want and deserve. It is not anyone else's responsibility to make you feel good about yourself, so don't use being an empath or highly sensitive as an excuse to be annoying, irresponsible, childish, and act like an ass.

Being empathic is how you process information, not an excuse to blame. The feelings you feel are yours. Others do not put them there. It is how you interpret the data and how your soul system guides you to the correct course. Your feelings are the built-in guidance system that tells you what is in or out of sync with your whole system. These senses are the greatest gifts to direct you away from unhappiness and into happiness. Your feelings and senses are the connection to your greatness and the greatness of the universe. When you learn about this part of you and how to navigate it, the world is your oyster, for nothing can or will stop you from being your highest self. If you are sensitive, learn about yourself. Learn how to manage your energy, thoughts, and emotions. Sensitivity is your superpower. Please don't give it away to nonsense, and don't give it away to others. Think of it as your bank account, and add to it daily. Before you know it, you will be wealthy in so many ways that my words cannot accurately express the joy and fulfillment you will feel.

So don't be an ass; be an asset to yourself, your family, and your global community.

CHAPTER 12

Things to Think About

LIFE IS NOT FAIR

Have you ever felt that life was not fair? Why? Because things didn't turn out the way you wanted or you thought that you were on the losing end of the stick? Does it seem like sometimes everyone else gets to win while you are constantly losing? How about the fact that sometimes things are just not equitable? I have experienced that myself many times. In the big picture, is it genuinely unfair, or am I seeing only a tiny portion of the bigger picture?

It depends on how you look at it. If I were to look at it from my ego or physical consciousness, life is unfair. Look at all the inequities in the world. They are everywhere. Every ethnic group, every race, every gender, every nationality, every religion, every society and economic background has something to say about this. I bet there isn't anyone reading this book who doesn't feel they have gotten screwed over somehow, but did you? Is it possible that life is fair, and inequitable situations show you that your mind is out of balance? To me, life is fair, but people aren't, and as long as people are not balanced, you will experience inequitable situations.

You see life as something that happens to you instead of seeing it as something you create. Life itself is perfect in every way. It is fair, it is just, it is kind, and it is without emotion. It is a matter of fact. It is energy, and for every action, there is a reaction. This life is kind and just, but it feels unfair if you don't understand it. If you see your life through your lumen mind, you will realize this and cherish the opportunity to balance your body and mind with your spirit. When you live only from your human mind, you can't understand this because you feel that life is happening to you. You don't think you have control, and you don't know the power within you to change it. Not realizing this keeps you stuck in being victimized and persecuted. In truth, you are not being either. You are showing yourself that you are out of balance and need to stand up for yourself more or speak up for what you want or deserve. I say *stand up* or *speak up* because I am not working on you but giving you a relative answer.

When you begin to evolve from your human to lumen mind, you understand that what you have created is for your balance and growth and has nothing to do with anyone or anything else. It is all about you and for you. It is the experience of your spirit in the physical realms.

So, next time you feel that life is unfair, consider that there is a more significant reason and allow yourself the chance to bring it to balance. It is effortless to do once you know how, and you will feel empowered knowing that you are controlling life and it is not controlling you.

WHAT WOULD JESUS DO? (WWJD)

About twenty-five years ago, when I was living in Arizona, it was common to see people wearing WWJD bracelets. For those of you who are not familiar, *WWJD* stands for *What would Jesus do?* What would Jesus do? Are you kidding me? It should say WWYD. What would you do? What would you do if you were in this situation? Would you be kind? Would you be compassionate?

Would you look at yourself and ask yourself why or how you got into this situation and what you will do to escape it? Why are you asking what would Jesus do? If you wear the bracelet, you already know what he would do. I may be splitting hairs here, which is semantics, but my point is to look to yourself. Be responsible, be accountable, and be present. I understand and respect the teachings of Jesus, but it is two thousand years later. Can't you give the guy a break and take on a little more responsibility? If so, ask yourself what your responsibility is next time.

TURN THE OTHER CHEEK, AND YOU'LL MAKE YOURSELF SICK

Turning the other cheek is not turning the other cheek. Many of you want to do the right thing and be the bigger person in some situations. I know that you want to follow the teaching of Jesus, the Bible, or your religion, but when you turn the other cheek without resolving the issue you have in the first place, all you are doing is making yourself sick. It would be best if you only turned the other cheek when you have evolved enough to know why the person or situation has you upset and can rise above it in a way that you understand and can be compassionate about.

A woman in one of my classes talked about turning the other cheek because she was the better person in the relationship between her and her ex-boyfriend. When I asked her if she had resolved the issue, she said yes, but I could tell her blood was boiling. How have you resolved the issue? What have you learned about yourself that made you understand their position? She had no answer. I asked her if she still felt attacked or wronged by this person. She said yes. I asked, "How did you resolve it then?" She said she turned the other cheek. "Oh, I see. You turned the other cheek by sweeping it under the rug and ignoring it." "Yes, she said. I am the bigger person." I asked, "How does that make you feel?" "Angry," she said. "Well, you didn't turn the other cheek then, did you?" "No, I supposed I didn't."

She understood her anger for him was eating at her, and she couldn't move on until she resolved the pain. She started Mindkeeping and was already feeling better within a week or two. She was able to see her role in the relationship, as well as where and why they weren't compatible. What had started as pain and anger soon turned into wisdom and understanding. Within weeks, she could forgive him and herself and move peacefully into her future. That's the definition of turning the other cheek.

WHY LOVE CAN BE A BAD THING

Everybody wants to be loved, but that is only sometimes a good thing. Why? It's not love itself that is bad but the interpretation of love that screws it up. There are too many interpretations of love. Every person, place, or thing has a belief in what love is. It is too broad a brush and overused in its crappy content to be accurate or adequate.

Examples: "He hits me, but he loves me." Is that love? No. Not in my book. That is abuse. "I love animals," said the hoarder, who had five dead cats and a dog buried under their garbage. Is that love? No. Not in my book. "I love my God, so I kill for him." Is that love? No, not in my book. "I love you, but I will do whatever I want regardless of whether it hurts you." Is that love? No, not in my book. Because this is my book, I will tell you what I believe to be the answer to this love dilemma: *kindness*. Replacing love with kindness would create a much better interpretation and intended meaning for love. You can all relate to kindness. You have all had a kindness done to you or did one for someone else. Kindness always feels good. It is without conditions. It is universal. The interpretation is uniform by almost everyone. It is love in pure form.

When you go on a date or are ready for a new relationship, ask yourself, *Is this relationship kind? Is this person kind to me and me to them?* If not, move on. Ask yourself at work. *Am I being kind to myself working here? Or is there something better for me?* In your family life. *Am I being kind to myself, my spouse, or my kids?* If not, correct your course.

Don't use the word *love* as a way to settle. "I love them, so it's good enough." Is it good enough, or is it an excuse not to deal with the issues that bother you? You will never know until you ask yourself, *Is it kind?*

WHY IT'S NOT BETTER TO GIVE THAN RECEIVE

If you are like most red-blooded Americans, you have learned that it is better to give than to receive. Right? So, what's the problem? The problem is you give and give until you have nothing left to give. Life is about balance, and everything in life is a relationship. It is a relay whether with yourself, your family, your career, or your finances. A give-and-take to create balance. You create an imbalance in your system when you give and don't receive. Of course, there are times when you make a conscious choice to give, knowing that it is not reciprocal. That's OK. I'm not suggesting that you stop giving. Look at it from a more balanced perspective. For instance, my sister always says nobody goes to their grave wishing they worked another day in their life. How many of you are working way more than is necessary? Are you working and not being compensated?

My oldest son is an excellent example of this. He said, "Mom, I'm tired of working sixty or seventy hours a week and only getting paid for forty. My time is valuable, and if my employer doesn't compensate me, I no longer want to work there." To remedy the problem, he decided to go from a salaried employee to freelance in his career, in which he gets paid for all hours over forty. He doesn't have the title of his salaried position, but he has more time and money. He feels more balanced and is much happier than he was before.

How about relationships? Are you the one who is always giving? Are your relationships give and take or give and give? If it is give and give, it is only a matter of time before that becomes an imbalance, causing you to feel angry, resentful, or manifest an illness of some kind. Remember, relationships of any kind are a relay of energy. Think of it like a game of catch. You aren't playing catch if you keep throwing the ball and nobody throws back. You are just throwing a ball that you have to retrieve. There is no balance in that. It is one-sided. Find the balance. Receive what you need, put your needs first, and then share equitably with others. Notice that I have changed the words *give and take* to *share*. *Give* and *take* seem proprietary as *sharing* feels more mutual.

What do you have to share, and what do you want others to share? Let's go back to my son. He shares his time and knowledge to complete the job for his employers. They, in turn, share their money and benefits with him. Most of the time, this will be an equal relay, and sometimes, it will be in favor of one another; however, the more equitable your relationships become, the more they will balance out in the end.

I CAN'T HEAR WHAT YOU ARE NOT SAYING

Feeling unheard is a common theme with many of my clients. It doesn't matter if they are male or female; they have a problem speaking up for themselves. It's not that they don't want to. They don't know how to or are afraid to. They feel it is better to keep peace than rock the boat. However, they are the ones getting the short end of the stick. Sometimes, they are angry because they are not getting what they deserve. Be it at work or home, they suffer in silence.

As I work with them to correct this issue, I remind them that nobody can read your mind. If you want a change, you have to initiate it. You can't expect someone to know what you want or what makes you angry. You have to have a dialogue. Going back to the relay in relationships, it is a give-and-take. You express what you want, and they can choose to comply. Many times, I hear, Well, it doesn't matter." Yes, it does matter, or you wouldn't have brought it up. It matters because you matter. If you don't think what you feel and want matters, then you are on the road to disappointment.

Disappointment sucks. Nobody wants to be disappointed, but you allow it to happen by putting your wants and needs in someone else's hands. Don't get me wrong. It takes practice to speak up. If you are old-school like me, you know children should be seen and not heard, don't talk back, and respect your elders. I am all about respecting people, but at what price?

People need to know what you want. You have to tell them, which creates the risk of being knocked down or rejected. It doesn't have to be complicated. Start with something simple, like what do you want for dinner? Don't say "I don't care" if you do. Speak your mind. If whomever you are with wants pizza but you want Chinese, tell them, "I'm not feeling the pizza; How about Chinese?" That person might not like that either, but you can talk to each other until you find something suitable for both of you.

It is a lot more complex in long-term relationships because you have each played roles for so long, and when you change that role, it changes the relationship's dynamic. Most times, it is good, but sometimes it could be better. Usually, when that happens, it is because you have different agendas or have outgrown the relationship.

If you are starting to date, be mindful of what you want in a partner. Don't just accept a warm body. Put some parameters and boundaries in place. Have specific criteria while being realistic. It's not likely that Brad Pitt will walk into your office and fall in love with you. Not that it can't happen, but it won't, primarily if you work for an orthodontist in Queens and Brad lives in Hollywood. Be realistic. Be honest. I have had this conversation with my daughter numerous times because she ran down the rabbit hole of not speaking up. She did not like conflict and avoided it at every turn. This avoidance created a crap storm of heartache and drama for her. In short, she wanted to get married and start a family. She was so focused on getting married and starting her family, she left out the most important detail: her. Within the next six months, she had moved, married, and was pregnant. She soon realized that this wasn't the guy for her. He was terrible for her. One thing led to another and another, and after three years, a toddler, a car repossession, ruined and stolen credit, and landing on the brink of bankruptcy, she finally moved on.

She allowed all that to happen for two reasons. First, she was so focused on starting her family that she was unaware of what was good and healthy for her. The other reason was she didn't speak up. She tried but felt he twisted the conversation and put all the blame on her. She didn't like the conflict, so she backed down, allowing him to have his way. It was a game of cat and mouse in which she was the mouse who didn't want the conflict. The conflict felt uncomfortable, so she avoided it. She stayed in a bad relationship because she didn't speak up.

The problem is not only a need for speaking up but also picking the wrong partner. Sometimes, people choose partners that they feel are authorities over them or that they have to help or fix. They don't choose partners that are equal to them. If you choose someone who is on the same wavelength as you, then they will gladly make adjustments to the relationship. They want to make you happy, and you want to make them happy, but not at either's expense but in a way that is complimentary to both.

Again, you have to know what you want to know what to ask for. A student said she didn't like the people she worked with because they didn't listen to her. I asked, "What did you say that they didn't respond to?" She said, "I didn't say anything, but you would think they would be more considerate of this or that." I said, "How would they know?" She didn't have an answer. I said, "I'm confident they would gladly accommodate you if you pulled them aside and explained what you wanted and why you felt this way." It took her a few weeks to get up the courage, and when she finally asked, they were glad to make the necessary adjustments. It's not that they didn't want to listen to her; they didn't know it bothered her.

When your children are learning to speak, you encourage them to use their words instead of pointing. You, too, need to use your voice to communicate what you need to make you happy because only a few people are actual mind readers.

THE LAW OF ATTRACTION

What is the law of attraction? The law of attraction stems from the concept that like attracts like, positive or negative thoughts bring positive or negative experiences into a person's life. My students tell me they are constantly working on the law of attraction and putting out good thoughts so they can receive the good in return. I firmly believe in positive thinking, but the law of attraction is more complex than this.

Yes, the law is actual, as I have seen and experienced it. However, it does not work on thought or desire alone. Your thoughts may want one thing, but your emotional energy may be on a very different page. Mindkeeping is essential because it helps you recognize where your thoughts and emotions are out of alignment and how to put them back in sync. When they are in sync, the law of attraction will work for you intentionally and purposefully.

I say *intentional* and *purposeful* because the law is always at work in some way or another. Think of how many things you attract to you that you don't want. How many problems and disasters do you think you can or could avoid if you intentionally bring or reflect what you want or don't want into your life? Imagine your life when you know that you are the one who is creating all the good and all the bad by how you think and feel. Doesn't it make you want to know more about how this energy can work for you?

If the law of attraction worked only on the energy, frequency, and vibrations of thought without regard to your emotions, you all would be millionaires. Any person who ever wanted to win the lottery would be a millionaire. Why aren't you? Because there is a misalignment between what you want and what you feel you deserve. Mental versus emotional.

When I say "know your frequencies, " I mean know what energies you hold on to regarding thoughts, beliefs, feelings, and memories. Most people need to learn what frequencies they are giving out and receiving. Not knowing is where the problems begin.

Your frequencies are like your cosmic calling cards. It's what you share with everything that exists, be it a person, place, or thing. It is your personal energy ID, and even though your mouth may be saying one thing, your frequencies may tell a different story.

Think of it as someone having a good vibe or a bad vibe. Sometimes, you like or dislike someone for no apparent reason. It is most likely because of the frequencies they are giving out that you are receiving. You want to learn to discern which is which, so you are only dealing with your energy and not being influenced unknowingly by someone else's frequencies.

Have you had the experience of walking into a place and getting the creeps? Have you been in a space that makes you feel uncomfortable? How about somewhere that makes you feel good? Maybe you don't know what it is about the place; it's just a feeling you have. All of this is energy, and what you feel is how you are interpreting the frequencies.

REJECTION OR RE-DIRECTION

Have you been snubbed by a friend or turned down by someone you liked? Did it seem devastating at the time, only to make you feel relieved down the road? Your lumen mind is always at work, even if you are not aware of it, and sometimes rejection is the best thing that could happen to you. I know it has been for me. There have been times that I wanted a promotion or job that I didn't get, only to find out later that I was better off not getting what I wanted. Was I rejected, or was I redirected? If you feel rejected, you feel bad about yourself. It may bring up insecurities of not being good enough or not feeling wanted, but when redirected, you are likely creating a better situation for yourself. You may not feel that way in the moment, but you understand the wisdom in time. There have been times when I didn't get the job I wanted, and I felt devastated until I found a better job that paid me more. I have had relationships that I wanted to work out, only to realize that, in the end, I dodged a bullet. Rejection is a good thing. It is a time to reflect, contemplate, and see where your energies are out of alignment.

Check your motive. *Is this what I want?* I had a student who felt rejected because she didn't get into a psychology program she applied for. After chatting for a few minutes, we got down to the nitty-gritty of her motive. She wanted to complete the program because she thought it would validate her work. She was already doing the work and didn't want to spend the extra time in school because it took her away from her goals. So, in reality, she wasn't rejected. She was redirected.

Everything changed when she saw the truth of what she wanted from a different perspective. The sting and stigma of feeling rejected changed to knowing she wasn't wasting time on something she thought she should do. Now, she could put the time into and focus on what she truly wanted.

FAITH OR FEAR

How many of you live your life in faith, and how many live in fear? Life is simple when you realize it is a series of choices, and the only two choices are faith or fear. What is faith? According to the dictionary, it is complete trust or confidence in someone or something based on spiritual understanding rather than proof. Do you live your life this way? If so, what do you have complete faith and confidence in? If you believe in God, do you trust it so much as never to have to feel fearful? I hear a lot of people say they believe in God. They go to church, and they are faithful. Yet they worry about everything. Others claim to be spiritual and trust the universe will care for them. But they don't realize they are the universe. How can you have faith in something if you don't know what it is? Do you have faith in God or the universe? Can you see, hear, touch, taste, or smell it? No. Can you feel it? Yes. So, faith is a feeling you have inside of you, just as fear is. If you have a feeling that makes you feel good and believe in what you can't see, doesn't it make sense that it is part of you?

Faith and fear. Two sides of a coin that both belong to you. It is your choice to choose to feel faithful or fearful. It is not God. It is not the universe. It is you. Your spirit connects to your soul, and your body determines your feelings.

It has always been you, and you are responsible for that. That is not to say that God/Universe/Source of energy isn't the primary benefactor of all that you are. Still, you individually choose to know yourself well enough to determine the degree of faith or fear you choose to have.

Fear is a waste of time and energy. It takes the focus off of you and puts it on something or someone else. It drains you of your energy and robs your mind of your intentions. Fear does almost nothing for you except to keep you safe or alert in times of danger. I also don't mean to discard common sense for fear, such as jumping off a building or doing something you know will harm you to test the fates. I am sincerely talking about being in a space within yourself that will always choose faith over fear because you trust yourself enough to know what you want will happen. Does that mean it will happen as you want in the desired timeframe? Hell no. It doesn't always work that way, but you will know that whatever is in store for you will be good and benevolent because you planned it that way. It is almost hard to imagine that life can be this simple, but it is.

The hard part is taking the time to know yourself. Getting to know you will be your biggest challenge and your most significant accomplishment. Just keep choosing faith even when you don't quite believe it. Before long, you will live in faith and never have to be paralyzed by fear again.

CHAPTER 13

Keywords

I don't know about you, but there have been so many times in my life that people would say something, and I had no idea what they were talking about. For instance, I was in a meditation class and instructed to center myself. Center myself how? What does that mean? Everyone seemed to get the memo but me, so I assumed I didn't understand it. It took me years to come to terms with usable definitions I could comprehend, and you may need clarification about it too. If you already know, that's great. If you need help, I put together a list you will want to keep handy on your spiritual journey.

Energy: Einstein said, "Everything is energy, and that's all there is to it. Match the frequency of the reality you want, and you cannot help but get that reality. It can be no other way. This is not philosophy. This is physics." Everything is energy, and all energy has vibrations that emit frequencies. Energy can have different forms, but for now, let's go with the reference of someone having high or low energy.

Vibration: All energy vibrates. Everything we see, touch, hear, smell, and taste is our interpretation of that vibration. We can feel a vibration, such as a guitar string or a cello chord, but some vibrations are so subtle that it takes empathy or instinct to feel. For instance, you may refer to it as a good or bad vibe. Ultimately, we want to be more consciously aware of the vibrations we are holding and the frequencies they are emitting.

Frequency: Frequencies determine and differentiate vibrational patterns of energy. All energy has a frequency. You have a set of unique frequencies too. Frequencies also have patterns.

For instance, floors or walls have a lower frequency and appear solid, but light, on the other hand, has a higher frequency, which is thinner and more transparent. It is essential to know what frequencies you are giving off because these are the ones you attract to yourself.

Thoughts and emotions have frequencies. When you pay attention to your frequencies, they help you determine what is in or out of sync within your energy fields. If the frequencies of your thoughts are low, your energy will be low. The higher the frequency, the happier you are because you are more aligned with your actual state of being, which is light.

Balance: To balance your energy, you want to create an equal distribution of your energies by putting yourself back into a state of neutrality. For instance, if you are angry, you want to move your thoughts and feelings from anger to happiness, creating a balance of peace. Like a pendulum, you don't want to go too far one way or the other but find the balance and resting place between the two opposing forces.

Center: To center is to focus and find the reference point within yourself that gives you the most incredible feeling of peace, tranquility, and sense of self. When you know yourself, you know your center and can always move back into that space no matter what is happening around you.

Chakra: *Chakra* is a Sanskrit word meaning "wheel" or "disk." They are spinning vortexes of nonphysical light energy within the body. You can feel them but not see them. The chakras run from the base of the spine to the top of the head. Each chakra has a corresponding color and function and contains the vital life force that keeps us alive and well.

Consciousness: Consciousness is a state of awareness. Seven levels of consciousness correspond with the seven chakras. The higher the consciousness, the more aware you are of yourself and your surroundings. The higher your consciousness, the higher your frequencies, creating healing and positive change.

Spirit: Nonphysical. It is the abstract aspect of us that is perfect and constant. It is not human, but it is part of humanity. You have a spirit, but you are a soul.

Soul: The soul is a collection of every thought, deed, action, feeling, memory, and belief played out on Earth. It is your personal experience within your body. Your soul is part of your physical and spiritual nature as the soul moves past the beliefs of its physical nature and recognizes that it, too, is spirit. Miracles happen.

Empath: An empath is a person with the heightened ability to understand another individual's mental or emotional state.

Highly sensitive person (HSP) A person with high mental, emotional, and social sensitivities but not necessarily an empath. Although you can be both an empath and highly sensitive, empaths take the sensitivity further by being able to absorb the energies of other people and places.

Clearing: Clearing is like cleaning the house and removing the old vibrations and frequencies you don't need. Clearing means removing or cleaning the lower-vibrational frequencies of your thoughts, emotions, beliefs, circumstances, home, and surroundings and removing those you may have picked up that don't belong to you. You can clear in many ways; however, the most common is to sage or smudge your body and surroundings to release old energies.

Grounding: A technique to reconnect you to the earth and to bring the nonphysical energy into the physical. Like a lightning rod. Grounding is calming and essential to staying focused in the body and the moment. It also helps bring creative ideas into clarity and focus.

Connecting: You are connecting the light consciousness of your spirit and soul with your physical consciousness to awaken your mind. The light activates the cells, DNA, and brain activity, releasing information stored within the body to help it heal.

Lumen consciousness: The next generation of consciousness, unified consciousness as opposed to dual consciousness. It is also known as universal consciousness or Christ consciousness.

Lumen being is a human being consciously aware of and actively striving to live from their higher unified consciousness.

Mindkeeper: A person who intentionally illuminates their mind to awaken, evolve and heal by expanding into higher levels of lumen consciousness.

The Power of YOU

You are Everything. You are the universe. You make all the good happen in your life, and you make all the bad happen, too. You are a frequency that is in harmony with other frequencies. You are a frequency that is in disharmony with other frequencies. What frequency are you? It depends. You are different frequencies at different times with different people under different circumstances. It does not matter when, where, how, or why; it always comes back to you. You are the creator of it all. You are the chief cook and bottle washer. You are the wizard behind the curtain that is you, and only you have the power to change it.

WOULD YOU LIKE TO KNOW MORE ABOUT BEING A MINDKEEPER?

Subscribe to my free newsletter at mindkeeping.com